MID-CONTINENT PUBLIC LIBRARY
3 0000 13239949 8

WITHDRAWN
FROM THE RECORDS OF THE
MID-CONTINENT PUBLIC LIBRARY

RABBITS

Gentle Hearts • Valiant Spirits

D1275149

Mid-Continent Public Library
15616 East US Highway 24
Independence, MO 64050

What others are saying about this book

These heartwarming stories about rescued rabbits and the people whose lives they touched are sure to provide, as Cleveland Amory was fond of saying, "hope for the hopless." Rabbits are sometimes described as the animals God has forgotten, but Marie Mead remembers them with such warmth and passion that this book will teach us something about the merciful treatment we owe to rabbits and, indeed, to all creatures.

—MICHAEL MARKARIAN, executive vice-president of The Humane Society of the United States and president of The Fund for Animals

~

One doesn't have to share a home with a rabbit to enjoy this absolutely captivating collection of stories about the joys and tribulations of life with bunny. But I warn you: this book may make the idea of a rabbit companion rather tempting! *Rabbits: Gentle Hearts, Valiant Spirits* is above all about love, respect, compassion, and acceptance. It persuasively reinforces the depth of the animal-human bond while at the same time gently reminding us that, as guardians, we must be forever vigilant because caring for a pet is a lifelong commitment.

—SUSAN TAYLOR, executive director of Actors and Others for Animals

~

Rabbits: Gentle Hearts, Valiant Spirits educates, inspires, and charms us. But most importantly, it is a call to action. This important book helps us appreciate the special qualities of rabbits and motivates us to take responsibility, ensuring they are given the respect and care they deserve.

—MARY LOU RANDOUR, author of *Animal Grace* and director of the Department of Human-Animal Relations: Education and Outreach for The Humane Society of the United States

~

With great respect and appreciation, I bow to author Marie Mead. Through her compassion, dedication, and clarity of intent, she brings to light the magical and very real 'Beingness' of rabbits as sentient, courageous, and highly intelligent citizens of this planet. *Rabbits: Gentle Hearts, Valiant Spirits* adds a powerful boost to the emerging ethos that honors all life. Please read this book and give it to everyone you know.

—RITA REYNOLDS, author of *Blessing the Bridge* and *Ask the Cow*; editor of the quarterly journal, *laJoie*

One of the first steps toward developing care and compassion for animals is providing people with a better understanding of animal behavior and needs. Marie Mead's *Rabbits: Gentle Hearts, Valiant Spirits* takes this step through a series of heartwarming stories about individual rabbits who survive deplorable situations and the human companions who commit to helping them. Each page brings us closer to understanding the world of domesticated rabbits and increases our desire to ensure their well-being, now and in the future.

—JEANNE MCCARTY, executive director of REAL School Gardens

~

Rabbits: Gentle Hearts, Valiant Spirits is a wonderful tribute to domestic rabbits—to their uninhibited *joie de vivre*, endless curiosity, and wide range of expression. When allowed the time and space to develop their diverse natures, these extraordinary creatures lead humans into a magical world as interesting as *Watership Down*—but as reality, not fiction. If you don't believe that rabbits have individual and complex personalities to match our own, read this charming and insightful book.

—JEFFREY MOUSSAIEFF MASSON, author of *When Elephants Weep*, *The Pig Who Sang to the Moon*, and *The Face on Your Plate*

~

Marie Mead has done for rabbits what Jane Goodall has done for chimpanzees and Jeffrey Masson for farm animals. Pairing heartwarming true stories with clear, accurate, and concise information about rabbits' physical and emotional needs, this book shines a spotlight on their unique personalities. In story after story, rabbits reveal to their human companions their complex, always individual, temperaments. Rebounding from an often dire beginning, each rabbit demonstrates resilience, determination, and a tremendous capacity for giving and receiving love. This book will forever change the way we look at these remarkable creatures.

—JOANNE LAUCK (HOBBS), author of *The Voice of the Infinite in the Small* and founder and executive director of Catalyst for Youth, Inc. and Heart of Chaos

~

Marie Mead's collection of inspiring stories is truly enriching. I found myself experiencing a vast range of emotions as I read tales of amazing acts of acceptance and compassion. The stories prove that rabbits can be valuable teachers of life lessons and that there is no greater gift than unconditional love. Readers *of Rabbits: Gentle Hearts, Valiant Spirits* will gain a new respect for the strength of one of nature's most fragile creatures.

—ERIKA SMITH ROYAL, founder and president of Brambley Hedge Rabbit Rescue

The stories of Kali, Kumar, and the other bunnies touched me in a way that I had not expected—who would have thought that such tiny souls could be such powerful teachers. Kudos to Marie Mead for enlightening the public on the plight of rabbits through these enchanting and bittersweet stories.

—SUSANA M. DELLA MADDALENA, executive director of PetSmart Charities

~

Keeping a rabbit in a hutch—like keeping a dog tethered—is, unfortunately, too often a socially acceptable practice. *Rabbits: Gentle Hearts, Valiant Spirits* challenges the conditions in which many rabbits exist and presents both facts and true stories to encourage a more vital, interactive life with these intelligent animals. This book will change the way rabbits are viewed by many in our culture, moving us closer to a just, compassionate, and peaceful society.

—KENNETH SHAPIRO, PhD, editor of *Society and Animals* and executive director of Animals and Society Institute

~

As a busy exotic animal practice, our staff has witnessed both good and bad animal treatment—not unlike the accounts in *Rabbits: Gentle Hearts, Valiant Spirits.* I value this exceptional book both for the heartwarming stories and for the lessons it provides on how to create the best life possible with (and for) a house rabbit.

—ANGELA M. LENNOX, DVM Dipl ABVP-Avian, past president of the Association of Exotic Mammal Veterinarians

~

When I read the eloquent Foreword by Dr. Michael W. Fox, I wondered if the rest of this book could possibly measure up. It did. Beautifully written stories focus on the positive outcomes of animal rescue, celebrating individual lives saved. All participants in this book deserve congratulations—the people who were able to recognize and appreciate the intrinsic worthiness of their bunnies and the marvelous rabbits who brought out the best in their humans. *Rabbits: Gentle Hearts, Valiant Spirits* will strike a chord in everyone who cares about animals.

—MARINELL HARRIMAN, founder of the House Rabbit Society, author of *House Rabbit Handbook* and editor-in-chief of *House Rabbit Journal*

Rabbits: Gentle Hearts, Valiant Spirits is a most appropriate title for an engaging book that I couldn't put down! Each story is a learning experience, educating while tugging at our heartstrings. Marie Mead has captured the essence of these gentle and highly intelligent creatures, revealing their virtues as loving and wonderful companions. Animal lovers, teachers, and parents should surely read this book to understand the plight of one of the most misunderstood and overlooked of pets—the domestic rabbit.

—BARI MEARS, founder and president of the Phoenix Animal Care Coalition and coauthor of *Love Stories of Pets and Their People*

~

Rabbits: Gentle Hearts, Valiant Spirits will enchant all animal lovers. This collection of true stories—of rabbits' innocence and tenacity, courage and high spirits—offers readers a glimpse of the nature and needs of these gentle beings. As the adoptive parent of a rescued bunny, this poignant book touched my heart and spoke to my soul.

—KISKA ICARD, director of communications and marketing for the San Francisco Society for the Prevention of Cruelty to Animals

~

This book is a blessing for all rabbits and for all who love them. It offers a touching blend of heartwarming stories and practical guidance for proper care of our kindred spirits.

—ALLEN M. SCHOEN, DVM, MS, author of *Kindred Spirits*

Clay Myers

RABBITS

Gentle Hearts • Valiant Spirits

Inspirational Stories of Rescue, Triumph, and Joy

Marie Mead
with Nancy LaRoche

Foreword by Veterinarian Michael W. Fox, DSc, PhD

NOVAmaris
PRESS

Revised Edition

Copyright © 2007, 2010 by Marie A. Grosshuesch

All rights reserved. No part of this book may be used, reproduced, or transmitted in any form or by any means, electronic or mechanical, including photocopying, recording, or by any information storage or retrieval system, or stored in a database or retrieval system without the prior written permission of the publisher.

For information: Nova Maris Press, LLC, 977 Seminole Trail, #356, Charlottesville, VA 22901. www.novamarispress.com.

Marie Grosshuesch holds the copyright to all content in this book except for the writings listed below:
Foreword © 2007 Dr. Michael W. Fox
"Modeling Love and Respect for a Classroom Rabbit" © 2010 Cheryl Rosemary Abbott
"Drowned Rats" and "Frankie's Foible" © 2007 Nancy J. LaRoche
"Rabbit Teeth: The Importance of Proper Care" © 2007 Dr. Angela M. Lennox
"Emily" © 2007 Susan Chernak McElroy
"Born to Be *ME*!" © 2007 Bernie S. Siegel, MD
"Klezmer" and "The Rabbit Round-Up" are based on original stories by Caroline Gilbert that appeared in the Rabbit Sanctuary newsletter. They were rewritten with her permission.
Versions of two written pieces first appeared in issues of Joyce Leake's online-magazine, Living with Animals: Stories of People and Animals: "Love Your Rabbit" (June 2002) and "Lobo and Blueberry" (October 2002).
The photos and illustrations depict the actual rabbits in the stories, with the exception of the New Zealand white in "The Rabbit Round-Up."
"Jingle Bells," J. Pierpont, 1857.
"We Wish You a Merry Christmas," composer unknown, traditional.
"If wishes were horses," traditional proverb and rhyme.

Mead, Marie.
Rabbits : gentle hearts, valiant spirits : inspirational stories of rescue, triumph, and joy / Marie Mead ; with Nancy LaRoche ; foreword by Michael W. Fox. — Rev. ed.
p. cm.
Includes bibliographical references and index.
LCCN 2009922064
ISBN-13: 978-0-9786226-1-9
ISBN-10: 0-9786226-1-8

1. Rabbits—Anecdotes. 2. Human-animal relationships —Anecdotes. 3. Animal welfare—Anecdotes. I. LaRoche, Nancy, 1941- II. Title.

SF453.M378 2010 636.932'2
QBI09-320

Edited by Karen Pauba Witzke
Design by Rudy J. Ramos
Cover photographs by Velly Oliver
Printed in China

Dedication

This book is a tribute to Kali and her dearest rabbit friend, Kumar.
The two are treasured and inspiring beings who have brightened my life
in immeasurable ways.

Many other rabbits have played an important role, among them: two Angora rabbits, Muffin
and Milly; a lonely Holland lop named Kirby; steadfast partners, Prancer and Rosie;
a courageous little rabbit named Trooper; intrepid bunnies Siobhan and Oscar-Schneidig;
and the sweet, plucky Little Lord Fauntleroy.

Bill Reed Photography

Kali and Kumar

Velly Oliver

Contents

Acknowledgments xv
Author's Note xviii
Foreword *contributed by Dr. Michael W. Fox* xix
Introduction xxiii

Stardust 1
About Rabbits: deafness 9
Kali's Prince 10
About Rabbits: prey animals 13
Lovable Bobka 14
About Rabbits: litter box training 17
Emily *contributed by Susan Chernak McElroy* 18
About Rabbits: their true nature 22
A Real Head-Turner 23
About Rabbits: backyard hutches 27
Three Stately Ladies, One Noble Baron 28
About Rabbits: making friends 31
Interiors by Taz 32
About Rabbits: when a bunny's furred friend dies 36
The Tilted Butterfly 37
About Rabbits: a bunny's body—and handling 41

Frankie's Foible *contributed by Nancy LaRoche* 42
About Rabbits: creating a trusted friendship 45
A Treasure Found 46
About Rabbits: vision 49
The Rabbit MaMaa Triumphant 50
About Rabbits: reproduction 53
Born to Be *ME! contributed by Bernie S. Siegel, MD* 54
About Rabbits: rabbits as Easter gifts 59
Bunzo 60
About Rabbits: before bringing a bunny home 63
The Valiant Voyager 64
About Rabbits: their social nature (and binkies) 75
Pretty Ballerina 76
About Rabbits: issues of overweight 78
The Hidey Box 79
About Rabbits: non-bunny companions 83
Bunny's Christmas Kingdom: Joy Uncaged 84
About Rabbits: holiday concerns 88
Wily, Rascally Dave 89
About Rabbits: in a school classroom 91
Lobo and Blueberry 92
About Rabbits: children and bunnies 95
Klezmer 96
About Rabbits: carnivals and other public venues 99
The Rabbit Round-Up 100
About Rabbits: abandonment 105

The Priceless Tulip 106
About Rabbits: bunny-proofing the house 109
Brown Beauty 110
About Rabbits: benefits of spaying and neutering 114
Ramona 115
About Rabbits: cancer 118
Drowned Rats *contributed by Nancy LaRoche* 119
About Rabbits: keeping a bunny clean 122

Afterword: So You're Thinking about Getting a Rabbit. 123
Love Your Rabbit: The Basics of Rabbit Care 124
Rabbits + Classrooms = *Mismatch* 126
Modeling Love and Respect for a Classroom Rabbit
contributed by Cheryl Rosemary Abbott 132
Veterinary Care: Rabbit Basics 140
Rabbit Teeth: The Importance of Proper Care
contributed by Dr. Angela M. Lennox 144
Special Thanks 146
Authors 146
Artists 147
Photographers 148
Organizations 149
Resources 152
Index 156

Velly Oliver

Acknowledgments

Many people were involved with the creation of this book, and I wish I could write a paragraph about each of them. In many cases, I can only provide a listing of names, which does not do justice to the contributions made.

The rabbit, Kali, entered my life thanks to Judy Anderson and stimulated the creative glimmer that ultimately became this book. As the idea began to take form, Kay Fritzsche acted as my sounding board and Rosario Martinez-Cañas offered her seemingly unlimited creative vision. Joyce Leake published two of my stories as well as an article (each illustrated by Sarah Skeen) in her online magazine, and the favorable response to those endeavors provided additional impetus.

My dream of writing a book about rabbits took flight the day Susan Chernak McElroy, a favorite author, wrote to say that she would be happy to contribute a story. That marvelous news was followed by an uplifting message from agent Andrea Hurst, saying Dr. Bernie Siegel would love to have Smudge's story included.

The effort was further boosted by the friendship and support of Faith Maloney, a founder of Best Friends Animal Society; Caroline Gilbert, founder and manager of the Rabbit Sanctuary; and Erika Smith Royal, founder and president of Brambley Hedge Rabbit Rescue. Members of the Colorado House Rabbit Society provided information about some of their wonderful rabbits, and this revised edition also includes a story about a rabbit rescued by the Minnesota Companion Rabbit Society.

Encouraging words came from others as well. Joanne Lauck, whose friendship and work I greatly value, helped in countless ways. Author Amelia Kinkade and Michael Markarian, executive vice-president of The Humane Society of the United States and president of The Fund for Animals, offered inspiring thoughts and support. T. J. Banks and Rita Reynolds, authors and fellow animal lovers, did the same. Others who deserve mention include: J. Kirby Bivans,

Max Bruce, Ann Cahoy, the late Mary Ann Capra, Dr. Gabriel Cousens, Maggy Cuesta, Kristin Des Marais, Jasmine Estrada, the late Nathania Gartman, Anna Horton, Dr. C. Yashpal Jayne, Dr. Beverly Joyce, Dr. Terry Moore, Diane Young, and Liga Zvirgzdina.

As the process unfolded, Kali remained my constant inspiration, and many wonderful veterinarians and rabbit-knowledgeable people assisted me in caring for her. Dr. Jerry LaBonde was our primary support during the first difficult months. We were also very fortunate to work with other skilled veterinarians: Drs. Paula Bumpers, Laura George, Bill Guerrera, Donald Holmes, William Kurmes, and Dave Nicholson. Others who provided healthcare assistance include Pam Beets, Karen Green, Dana Krempels, Bea LeNoir, and Kathleen Wilkens. I'll always be grateful to Sue Green for putting me in touch with Connie Conine, whose knowledge of rabbits and background in occupational therapy proved invaluable.

I was delighted when Nancy LaRoche shared her love and knowledge of rabbits by contributing two stories and agreeing to collaborate on the project. Her excellent suggestions elevated the quality of the stories. I was very pleased when Cheryl Abbott agreed to contribute to this revised edition a thoughtful article about hosting a rabbit in the classroom. In addition, it was a great pleasure and privilege to work with the generous individuals who shared information about their rabbits, each mentioned at the beginning of the corresponding story. I am also sincerely grateful for the contributions of each of the talented artists and photographers credited throughout the book, including Beverly Endsley, who supports rabbit rescue in myriad ways.

Valuable suggestions from the pre-publication readers improved the text, and I thank Joan Carstensen, Dee Heinrich, Lucile Moore, Kay Pfaltz, Linda Seeman, Kathy Stevens, Susan Gossman Stevens, and Kay Wilhite. A sincere note of thanks for the thoughtful input that also came from Sandi Ackerman, Brenda Cullum, Nora Ernst, Edith Hathaway, Anita Kerr, Pam Laverty, Gary Loewenthal, Christine Schrock, Howard Voeks, Victoria Walton, and Alissa Witzke. I deeply appreciate James Wallace, president of the Society for the Preservation of English Language and Literature, for supporting the book and sharing his considerable literary knowledge.

In addition to Margo DeMello and Marinell Harriman, the following veterinarians offered their extensive knowledge, helping to make this book more accurate and complete: Drs. Wendy Asato, Vittorio Capello, Thomas Chlebecek, Hillary Cook, and Bill Guerrera. Dr. Angela Lennox provided professional advice as well as contributing an educational article.

The stories and educational pieces became what they are through the efforts of Karen Pauba Witzke. Her respect for animals as well as her knowledge of the English language are apparent on every page. Working with her was a real pleasure, and I am very grateful for her precision, style, and friendship.

That Dr. Michael W. Fox agreed to write the Foreword to this book is a heartfelt honor. His were the first books

I read when searching for answers about the behavior of a rescued cat, and he continues to be an inspiration to me. Dr. Fox's compassion, respect, and love extend to all beings and are very evident in his work.

Andrea Hurst was my literary consultant, and I appreciate her professionalism, patience, and humor. Designer Rudy Ramos created a beautiful book and made the process easy and enjoyable. Lloyd Rich gave important legal guidance, Janet Crownover provided computer research, Sreedharan Vijayarangam shared printing expertise, and Dan Poynter's writings presented publishing information. Publicist Dottie DeHart bestowed humor and insight when it was greatly needed, and her staff provided support in myriad ways. Both Robin Bartlett and Jeanne McCarty offered marketing suggestions, and Linda Kranz shared a creative revisioning of the book.

I'm deeply grateful to the following individuals who read the manuscript and offered review comments: Susana M. Della Maddalena, Margo DeMello, Marinell Harriman, Kiska Icard, Dr. Elliot Katz, Amelia Kinkade, Joanne Lauck, Dr. Angela Lennox, Michael Markarian, Jeffrey Moussaieff Masson, Jeanne McCarty, Bari Mears, Mary Lou Randour, Tom Regan, Rita Reynolds, Erika Smith Royal, Dr. Allen Schoen, Kenneth Shapiro, and Susan Taylor.

I also have words of appreciation for my mother, Audrey Grosshuesch, who edited early versions of the stories. She honors diversity, models strength and courage, and offers unfailing love and support. Additionally, I give thanks for my father, the late Donald Grosshuesch, who recognized and loved Kali's tremendous spirit and independence; my uncle, Vernon Wernecke, who understands how important the animals are to me and remembers to ask about them; and John Mead, dear friend and fellow animal lover, whose support helped make my dream of writing about rabbits a reality.

My deepest expression of gratitude begins with God, the Source of all. At a time when we were not looking for or even wanting more companion animals, I was firmly nudged to say "Yes" to a rabbit in need. The inspiration to begin writing stories about rabbits came unexpectedly and repeatedly—and I could not disregard it.

The rabbit in need was Kali, who became my gift beyond measure. A small black bunny whose strong spirit belied her many physical challenges, Kali educated me about rabbits while adding so much richness to my life. I gratefully acknowledge this remarkable little being who changed my life and acted as the catalyst for this book.

Author's Note

None of the stories in this book refer to a rabbit's "owner," a term which suggests that companion animals are property—relegated to the level of things and dealt with according to our desires. Instead, the word "guardian" is frequently used, interspersed with "human companion" and "caregiver" when those words better fit the story.

"Guardian" captures the best parts of humans' relationships with other animals, implying that creatures deserve to be treated with respect, compassion, and love because all animals are sentient beings and have inherent value. A guardian protects his or her dependent companions, honors each animal's individuality, and properly provides for physical, social, and emotional needs during the animal's lifetime.

Reference the Resource (Services) section for source information on the Guardian Campaign.

Foreword

The first animal whom I ever learned to hold properly, and trust and love, was my little bunny rabbit named Thumper. He was a black-and-white Dutch dwarf, but he was huge to me, filling my arms as he relaxed, feeling through his body my trust and lack of fearful tension. He was a gentle rabbit, never once biting me for being a somewhat clumsy and not yet very empathetic four-year-old.

My father built a beautiful big hutch for Thumper and set it in the back garden, protectively against the rear wall of our garage. I fed my rabbit and cleaned his hutch every day, always talking to him about the important topics and questions that filled my young mind.

I do not remember how long he lived, but I do recall the morning when I found my bunny friend lying unresponsive on his side. The night before he'd been alive and full of frisk so I was bewildered, waiting for his ears to move and nose to twitch as I called his name. Being too afraid to put a hand on him, I probed Thumper gently with a stick, wishing his spirit to return to his lifeless form. When I did eventually touch him, he was cold and stiff as wood. That was my first lesson in death and loss.

Just days later, while in the garden lush with flowers and insects and still wondering about life and death and worried about where Thumper had gone, I had an experience that was quite a surprise to me at my young age. I was looking skyward, through the English-morning mist, when everything became bathed in light. I transformed into a tiny particle, no longer a separate entity but instead clearly connected to the whole of life. I could feel Thumper's warmth and gentleness as he, too, was part of that infinite love and light. My fear of death departed, and my sense of who I was changed. I saw the world filled with other lives and forms of being, all distinctly joined to me and to one another and, thanks to a small rabbit, I saw them with great clarity and with everlasting awe. That experience has stayed fresh in my mind ever since because of what Thumper gave me in life and in death.

But though Thumper taught me such a profound lesson, it was wrong of us to have denied him any contact with his own kind during his life with us. He never had the chance to know what it is to be a rabbit and to be the soul-mirror of another in his form and state of mind. Rabbits, along with all other beings, have the right to live in harmony with their nature. They have a life and a will of their own, independent of our lives, interests, and needs.

I feel a terrible loneliness when I contemplate the existence and fate of millions of rabbits who live alone in tiny cages for their entire lives, unable to stretch out fully, move freely, or enjoy the life they were meant to have. Such treatment reveals our ignorance, callous indifference, and rabbit blindness. Whenever I think of this and about how disconnected we've become from nature, I fear what our children are learning. What is the likely outcome when we, as adults, model a lack of awareness of the inherent value of other creatures and a lack of concern about the quality of their lives?

Most of us would agree that pets have the right to a good home. But rabbits are unlike the cats and dogs with which we are so familiar, and our lack of knowledge too often means that the rabbits' needs are ignored. They were meant to live with other bunnies, playing all kinds of inventive games of speed and deception, determining their rank, engaging in grooming rituals, and caring for one another. Though selective breeding has made them less fearful and also dependent upon humans for safety and care, domestic rabbits can still enjoy warren life, though their "warren" may look quite different from that of a wild rabbit and may include, in addition to bunny companions, a human, cat, and dog. When humans establish a participatory relationship with their rabbits, they come closer to experiencing harmony with their essential self and all of the living earth.

Some of the beauty of my pet bunny is reflected in the beauty of this book, in the personal stories of human discovery, of living with rabbits, and of a rabbit's true and wonderful nature. As you will read, they are highly sociable, communicative, empathetic, intelligent, responsive, and readily trainable. The sciences of ethology and biology have helped deepen our understanding and appreciation of rabbits, and this important book takes us one step further. The intimate accounts of people's experiences with rabbits, which could never be replicated in a research laboratory, bring to conscious realization all that a rabbit is.

I urge you, when reading this book, to think about the suffering and deaths of untold numbers of rabbits who, every year, are used to test cosmetics, deodorants, and other products. No animal should ever be made to suffer partial blindness in testing a new mascara or to die from cancer because we refuse the wisdom of organic agriculture. There are many safe, natural, organic botanical products, including medicinal ones, readily available on the open market that do not victimize these creatures.

I believe that an animal-exploiting consumerism, which I equate with the inability to see the value in all life, must be replaced by a change of heart—opening to the angelic innocence of rabbits, knowing them as unique individuals, and seeing reflected in their eyes the ancient depth of being that moves us to realize the sanctity of all life.

Rabbits and other animals provide a link with nature, nourishing our own souls. In the wild, they are vital contributors to the health of eco-systems—meadows, grasslands, heaths, moors, steppes—being in co-evolved, mutually enhancing symbioses with the ground vegetation and, therefore, with the dependent insect, bird, and reptile populations. On many organically certified farms, rabbits and other furred, feathered, and scaled beings are welcome participants in the endeavors of my human friends and associates who are able to see as Thumper taught me to see. Together, they give CPR to the Earth—conservation, preservation, and restoration.

The worldview of rabbits is revealed in some detail in this book, along with the rabbit's basic environmental, social, and emotional needs. This will go a long way to enhance our respect for rabbits as feeling beings, who are in many ways more similar to us than they are different. In addition, because some people need to be educated toward greater empathy and others need to be educated toward greater responsibility, the information in this book will also help improve the care rabbits receive from their not-always-well-informed humans.

We can learn much from rabbits, if we but take the time to observe and learn. They are sensitive beings who are uninhibited and honest in their emotions and responses, and we would do well to emulate such authenticity.

Flash an intense light on a rabbit and she will freeze, an easy target for the hunter. Flash the light on how we humans mistreat other living beings and we also freeze. Let us flash the light in a new direction, as a beacon toward a more compassionate age—one in which this book, Thumper, and all animals can teach us how to live in connection with all life.

Humility, compassion, respect, and reverence for all living things are the keys to a just, humane, and sustainable society. It is time to move and to embrace the whole of Creation.

— Veterinarian MICHAEL W. FOX, DSc, PhD, BVetMed, MRCVS

Velly Oliver

Introduction

Her name was Kali, and she taught me lessons that transcended my usual boundaries. She happened to be a rabbit.

My important life lessons have often arrived in an unexpected manner, and most of the teachings have come from animal-friends. So it was with Kali.

She was a small rabbit, weighing less than four pounds. From the moment she arrived in our home, Kali commanded my attention. She'd been removed from a preschool classroom, where she suffered neglect and had become very ill. And yet she brimmed with personality, confidence, and self-will.

I was instantly captivated and promised Kali I'd do my best to provide good care. Though my husband, John, and I had rescued many abused and injured animals, she was the first with such permanent and extensive needs. Caring for Kali became a special gift—a perfect conduit for my development on the sometimes-arduous journey toward personal wholeness. I had to think and do things differently, to turn inward and find creative ways to help her overcome hurdles. In doing so, I overcame some of my own.

At the time, my father was in declining health. He and I had a close—though difficult—relationship. Through working with Kali, I came to truly know compassion, empathy, and wonder. Although I thought I was already aware of the depth and meaning of these life-enhancing emotions, I soon realized that I had only touched their surface. Kali opened me to the intensity of those feelings; because of her I began to understand and interact with my aging father on a much deeper level than would have been possible otherwise. In short, what I learned from Kali made me a more sensitive and respectful person.

As I tended her, I pondered the very different lesson the impressionable children at the preschool had inadvertently learned: that it was okay to neglect and mistreat a classroom pet. My concerns led to writing an article (appearing at the back of this volume) discussing the divergent needs of children and rabbits. That effort was the beginning of the process that ultimately created this book.

While researching rabbits in order to understand Kali and her needs, I learned about the plight of many domestic rabbits: neglected in small cages or backyard hutches, living without companionship, and often abandoned or euthanized because of a lack of understanding about their temperament and needs.

In sharp contrast, I met people who loved rabbits and who were willing to share their living spaces in ways that allowed the companion rabbits to express their true natures. Those were the people who smiled knowingly whenever I shared something special about Kali.

I wanted to collect information and write stories about those rabbits, the ones who were given freedom and allowed to exhibit the full panorama of their intricate personalities. I queried rescue organizations—dedicated folks who help educate others about the temperament and care of rabbits—for details about their rabbits. I also contacted Susan Chernak McElroy and Dr. Bernie Siegel, both of whom generously agreed to contribute to the project. And I wrote "Stardust" to capture Kali's story, including what a blessing she has been in my life. This book contains many of those stories. Even though some of the rabbits portrayed in the following pages endured sad beginnings, all the bunnies ended up in wonderful homes, living very happy lives.

I had planned to give Kali a copy of "her book" (as I've always considered it) even though I know she would have simply turned it into a napping spot. But just before the original edition of this book could be printed, Kali let me know it was time for her to depart this life. She remains in my heart, and she visits me during quiet contemplation and in my dreams, always demanding my attention. Other times I imagine her sitting on my late father's lap, reading together—the idea brings me quiet joy.

I continue to be amazed and humbled by what I have learned from rabbits, small unassuming creatures that they are. In truth, Kali was small in physical size only. She graced my life with her formidable presence, allowing me to grow in wisdom and strength. What I learned from her emphasizes the unity of all life and transcends the barriers that too often exist between humans and various species of other animals.

Kali remains my teacher and inspiration. She is not the only rabbit who has shared our household, but she was my first and she has blessed my life in numerous ways. For each moment with her, I am grateful.

—Marie Mead

Stardust

I wasn't expecting *her*.

I'm not sure who or what I was expecting, exactly—maybe a familiar rabbit from my childhood: the wild brown ones with cotton-ball tails and cute upright ears, who danced through grass fields decorated with clover and raced ahead of me in corn fields where I played hide-and-seek.

Those were the rabbits of my youth, and I knew back then that the very act of witnessing their *aliveness* would bring me luck. Each full moon I'd watch, hoping to glimpse one of them leap into the air, stardust trailing behind as she carried my dreams to the heavens.

On those visions hinged my presumptions about all rabbits, including the domestic rabbit for whom we agreed to provide a home.

My husband, John, and I had twenty-four hours to prepare for his arrival. We were told we'd be receiving a healthy six-month-old male rabbit with "behavior problems." He had been dismissed from a preschool classroom after lunging at a child who was trying to pet him through the wire cage.

We knew nothing about living with a domestic rabbit, so I did some quick preparations: found a rabbit veterinarian, obtained dietary guidelines, and checked out the two available library books. An expeditious shopping trip, a rapid perusal of the books, and we were as ready as we would be. At least the rabbit would be young and healthy—that meant there would be time to research and learn as we went along.

His arrival at 7:00 p.m. kicked holes in any expectations I might have had. Instead of a sleek brown rabbit with upright ears, the small cage held a black, long-haired rabbit with lop ears partially shielding dull, expressionless eyes.

I kept looking for the *aliveness*—but there didn't seem to be any. No fire, no vigor, not a glimmer of hope. Definitely no stardust.

Afraid to touch him and unable to voice my concerns, I simply stared. Surely there was some mistake.

But there wasn't.

A horrid, sinking feeling settled in my stomach. This was not the rabbit I was expecting. He was anything but healthy. Or happy. His very *essence* was missing.

The long Angora fur, thin and lackluster, hid his feet and belly. I thought I should pick him up and check his body—for lumps, bumps, *something.* Caution immediately intervened: *Be careful. You know virtually nothing about rabbits. You might injure him.* I had read enough to know that, if held improperly, injuring him was a probability, and a high one at that.

What was the matter with him? John and I kept staring, trying to discern any problems. As rabbit novices, we would have recognized only glaring health issues, and we saw nothing of the sort.

We couldn't help but *smell* a problem, though. A terrible stench had accompanied the bunny into the house, so we turned our attention to the wire cage—his "home" at the school—filthy with hardened diarrhea and urine.

After guiding him into a clean cat carrier, we discarded soiled cedar shavings; pried feces off the wire; sanitized the cage; scrubbed the slime-filled water bottle and food container; and threw out the unhealthy mix of green cereal, dried beans, and seeds. Then we put a cotton towel over a portion of the wire floor and ushered him back into his cage.

"After we get home from the vet's office tomorrow, I'll go shopping for the best rabbit house available," I promised.

There was no indication he heard me. But he did nibble the food purchased earlier that day, and we thought that was a good sign.

The next morning I waited with him for the animal clinic to open. It didn't take long for the veterinarian to complete the exam and give me the shocking news: we had rescued a two-and-a-half-year-old female bunny.

And she was dying.

"Her condition is so critical that even with medication and hydration she may not recover," the veterinarian advised. "She's severely malnourished, underweight, and in severe pain."

That wasn't all. Our new family member had a serious bladder infection and exhibited signs of gastrointestinal stasis, a painful killer of rabbits. As a result of living on a wire floor for so long, she had broken toes; sores on the bottom of her misshapen feet; improperly growing toenails, some more than two inches long; and weak, undeveloped leg muscles. The phenols from the cedar shavings made her susceptible to respiratory and liver problems, while the strong ammonia fumes from her urine-soaked cage might create additional health concerns.

When pressed to give a prognosis, the vet conceded, "Perhaps a week."

I drove home in a daze. *The poor little rabbit is dying. How could someone not notice?* Those were the only coherent thoughts that drummed in my head. And then it dawned on me: *She was in pain; that's why she lunged at the child.*

I hated putting her back into that wire cage, but it was all we had. "Just a few more hours and you'll have a new house, one *without* a wire floor." It didn't matter how short a time she might live, John and I weren't about to let her remain in the cage that had so damaged her body.

By mid-afternoon, a three-story rabbit condo was set up in our living room, and our resident bunny was placed inside. John made a short, carpet-covered ramp so Kali, as we named her, could more easily enter and exit her new abode. He also attached a roomy pen to keep our fragile little prey animal safe until our cats accepted her as a valued member of the family.

Bill Reed Photography

As soon as John opened her door, Kali stumbled down the low incline, nipping my hand when I tried to assist her. Her withered muscles allowed no more than an uncertain lurching movement. But her spirit, previously imprisoned as surely as if an iron mantle had been clamped around it, soared—*aliveness* shone from Kali's black-brown eyes. Her body tired quickly, but her eyes remained bright.

However, when we closed her inside her new house, to ensure her safety while we slept, Kali underwent a dramatic change. She began banging her head against the door, over and over. Alarmed that she might injure herself, John opened the door; she immediately stopped, remaining in front of the opening.

He closed it again, knowing we couldn't take the chance that one of our cats might harm her.

Kali again banged her head against the door. She didn't want out; she just didn't want to be shut in.

"We'll open it first thing in the morning," I assured her.

Kali's eyes lost their sparkle. She moved into a corner of her lodging, lay down, and turned her head away.

The aliveness was gone; it was as though we were watching her die.

Perhaps we were, and it frightened me.

Kali's misery was like a lead weight, so heavy and tangible that it followed us to bed. Finally, unable to sleep, I returned to the living room and opened the door to her condo, reading and maintaining vigil until morning.

The next couple of days were the same. I scrutinized her movements, trying to find signs of improvement. But her condition remained critical.

As we passed the one-week mark, it seemed Kali was responding to the medical treatment, although she remained in serious condition, straddling life and death. I was in contact with respected veterinarians, with the House Rabbit Society, and with others who knew rabbits. Instead of a learn-as-we-go situation, John and I were getting a crash course in health crises and medical treatment. But we were willing and committed students.

On her good days, she refused to remain in her condo. I'd open the play area and let her roam the house, allowing her to exercise her weak muscles as much as possible. The cats recognized Kali's substantial and forceful spirit and, even though she could not hop or run, they would back away when she slithered her way across the room.

Three weeks passed, and she was still alive.

November segued into the holiday season. At almost six weeks, her legs strengthened and she began hopping, albeit in an unsteady fashion. She was a feisty little thing, applying her right to freedom no matter how often she ended up spread-eagle on the floor.

But all was not well.

New concerns continued to surface. It was as though we peeled away one layer of health problems only to reveal another.

Kali's long black coat was often soaked with urine. I knew urine burn could be a serious problem and tried all the standard methods for keeping an incontinent rabbit dry. The vet ruled out a recurring bladder infection. Others suggested that Kali either had a behavior problem or was stressed due to the cats.

Intuition told me it was neither.

I researched, including textbooks containing medical information about rabbits. Nothing enlightened me.

Then Kali intermittently began losing her balance. X-rays revealed an active case of arthritis in her pelvis and legs. Every movement was painful.

A course of anti-inflammatory drugs, and Kali was able to move more easily and to actually squat while urinating. She continued to falter and end up on her nose, but she was getting stronger—and more independent.

I was hopeful that Kali was healing.

But then, nearly two months after she arrived at our home, the incontinence returned, caused by an improperly working bladder sphincter. And, despite the management of her arthritis, her balance problems returned. She didn't have a bacterial or viral infection, so I wondered if her vision was impaired or whether the third eyelids, which would sometimes partially close, were the cause of problems.

Continued consultations with veterinarians were helpful: Kali suffered from anemia, improperly functioning third eyelids, and probable neuromuscular damage that would cause ongoing difficulties.

Her early living conditions were taking their toll.

The New Year arrived, with Kali thumping it in. *Thump, thump, thump.* I knew this behavior, which had escalated over the weeks, was a symptom, but I couldn't discover the cause.

Even though I worked from home and could provide regular care, it became increasingly difficult for me to tend Kali. John and I were managing her health issues, but there was still something else wrong, something not yet detected. I could feel it.

But I didn't know how to find it.

One morning her soft, black coat was dripping with urine. I had been able to keep her delicate skin dry up to this point, but the problem was worsening and I knew something had to be done before her skin became painfully inflamed and blistered.

Finally, I had to admit that being captivated by Kali and wanting to give her a home weren't enough. John and I just didn't know enough to tend a rabbit with so many special needs.

I feared we would have to relinquish her. The misery was a savage lock around my heart. "Kali, I don't know how to take care of you," I hiccupped between sobs.

I renewed my efforts at calling people, trying to find someone who would spend time at the house and teach me more. I remember one phone call in particular: after hearing about our situation, the person suggested it might be kinder to euthanize Kali.

Euthanize Kali?

I could barely comprehend the words. They were like metal shards colliding in my head.

Kali was stronger in spirit than anyone I knew. Sure, she had some physical limitations, but that never stopped her. I thought of her as perfect, despite her myriad health issues.

That night, Kali's spirit charged through the midnight silence and into my dreams.

Before I could stop her, she proudly leaped through the underside of puff-cheeked clouds.

I followed, afraid she might fall. But then my eyes saw as hers did, and I wasn't frightened for her anymore.

Kali hopped with certainty over the sea of clouds, to horizon's edge.

I was in awe. Her legs worked—she was frisking about like a young colt! THIS was her reality, one where there were no boundaries, no rules, no restrictions.

I watched from a distance, wanting to remain out of sight, afraid my presence might be an intrusion that would dispel the miracle.

Then Kali turned and looked right at me. I realized she had known I was nearby all the time. She seemed at ease with me.

She started to come toward me. An acrobat, she bounded through the heavens. I was so happy she was coming to me, and I opened my arms to receive her.

Just that quickly she leaped—

The frantic barking of neighborhood dogs yanked me back into the bedroom, wide awake.

What did my dream mean? Had Kali died during the night?

I raced into the living room. There she was, dark eyes sparkling.

I sat with her and answers began coming. I realized my fears for her had become obstacles in my way. John and I had rescued many animals before but never a rabbit, so I had not trusted my instincts.

But I *knew* and understood Kali. I loved her and wanted to keep her with us.

I made more phone calls, seeking answers. And they came, in the form of a wonderful and generous occupational therapist who had lived with a rabbit. Connie came to the house and observed Kali. She listened as I described patterns and the behaviors that seemed out of place.

Then she lay down on the floor with me to watch Kali move around. Connie immediately detected a slight imbalance in Kali's hind legs—one leg was doing a majority of the work. Because of the Angora fur it wasn't easy to see, but Kali's front legs weren't working properly either. Severely splayed, they were unable to support her weight and only helped steer about. When our intrepid rabbit came to rest, the forelegs became like fins, sliding back alongside her body.

This was something no one had seen before because Kali would always sit with her back legs pushed forward—a response to weak muscles and arthritis, we thought, but in actuality also a way to keep her front legs in place and to remain upright. Now Kali was strong enough to hold her body in position, revealing one strong hind leg, one weak hind leg, and two impaired front legs. That helped explain her balance issues and her ineffective stance when urinating.

Connie demonstrated simple exercises to help strengthen Kali's muscles—like holding my hand against one side of her body so that she'd have to lean differently—and provided simple, creative solutions for keeping fur dry while ensuring safe footing.

And then another perceptive person visited us. Karen's knowledge of rabbits made it easy for her to confirm what I already suspected: Kali was deaf.

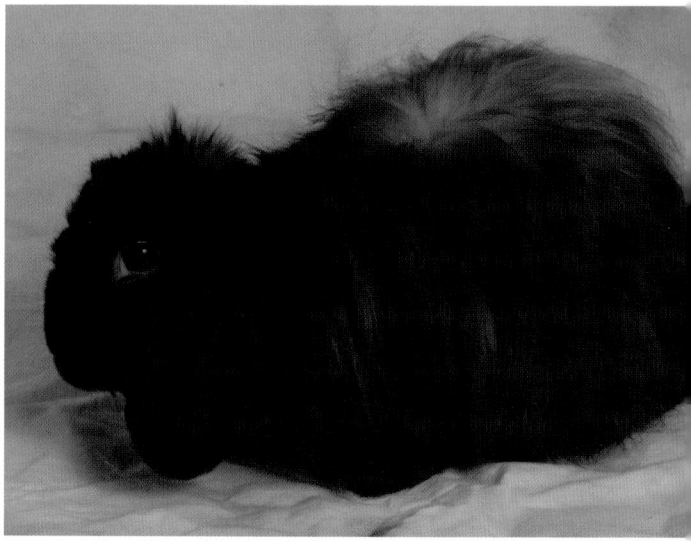

Bill Reed Photography

Ah, the last piece of the puzzle. Since Kali couldn't hear and because her vision was sometimes obscured by wayward third eyelids, she startled easily and thumped her distress.

Everything seemed so easy after that. No longer was I tentative when I needed to be assertive. I felt confident as John and I worked together to assist our precious rabbit.

Her muscles began to build; her back legs began working in tandem. She still hopped in an unsteady, lopsided fashion, but getting around was easier.

I started communicating with hand signals, and Kali responded.

She knew we were doing our best and began trusting us.

It was during this time that my father began showing serious signs of decline. His body, once strong, was aging rapidly. He shared his fears, especially about his memory loss, but I didn't have the knowledge—or patience at times—to assist him in all the ways he required. The fact that he resided in another state compounded the problem, so I arranged for others to accommodate his needs.

My life was just becoming routine again when, without warning, respiratory illness struck Kali. Her system shut down so quickly that she went into gastrointestinal stasis. I administered the prescribed medication, kept her body temperature stable, and hydrated and syringe-fed her, but death seemed imminent.

I held her, watching small breaths labor in and out.

Then she stopped breathing.

I did too. Tears streamed from my eyes. I wasn't ready to let her go.

I felt her body spasm. She started breathing again. Little short breaths, but she was breathing.

That night I had the same dream as before, but this time I saw the leap—

> *Kali started to come toward me. An acrobat, she bounded through the heavens. I was so happy she was coming to me, and I opened my arms to receive her.*
>
> *Just that quickly she leaped, stardust showering over me as she ascended to the stars.*

I startled awake. *Kali.* I hurried to make sure she was all right and was relieved to see her near-black eyes watching for me.

Kali gained enough weight to tip the scales at nearly four pounds. As she became stronger, she also came fully into her true self: a brave, spirited, dauntless, volitional, impertinent rabbit.

She was often indignant, even belligerent. If I was in her path, she would slap her tiny feet rapidly against mine, trying to get them to *move.* She'd give me a baleful stare and pull on my shoestrings if I happened to walk past empty-handed at feeding time. And if I dared sleep past 6:00 a.m., she would start thumping at regular, short intervals, then pick up her heavy food crock and bang it on the top platform of her condo.

She'd bite me if I held her too long—and some days, thirty seconds was too long.

Since she continued to progress, we had her spayed and, after healing, paired her with a gentle, neutered bunny. Kumar fell in love with Kali immediately and became her dearest and most comforting friend.

Things were looking up for our darling rabbit.

My father, on the other hand, continued a steady decline. But I found I was better able to assist him now. It was a revelation that Kali was the reason for my new attentiveness. Because of her I was able to think creatively about the care needed in special situations and was applying to my father what I had learned from a rabbit—an affirmation that life is, indeed, mysterious and wondrous.

I traveled back and forth to visit my father, learning valuable lessons from him and from Kali. As he became increasingly weak, she became increasingly strong. I shared stories about her, bringing a smile to his thinning face.

One year and nearly four months after coming to live with us, Kali ran for the first time. Her back legs had to do all the work, but she was fast, her long black skirt flouncing as she made her circuit.

Not long after that, she jumped fourteen inches to the top of a box, then insisted on getting down by herself. Before I could stop her, she did a nosedive, fortunately landing without harm.

She stood on her back legs, a lovely eight inches tall.

It was amazing to watch her. She was so alive! And independent. "Give me liberty!" was her demand whenever I held or groomed her.

Through it all, Kumar was her constant companion. When she'd tire, he would offer his body as a pillow, cushioning hers for as long as she needed, joining her when she had the energy to romp around the house.

When my father was well enough to be with us for the holidays, he met our rabbits and was immediately enchanted by Kali. From then on, he always asked about her—an endearing memory. It was easier to be lovingly patient with him now, because I had changed.

Kali has been a tremendous catalyst in my life—and a definite blessing. Because of her and the opportunities for learning that she provided, I've glimpsed selfless love, a lofty ideal I thought attainable only in my dreams. I gained a new level of compassion, which helped me to be gentle with my father and with myself. And even though my father is no longer on this earth, I still think of him when I share her stories, remembering his smile as I extol her compelling and valiant spirit.

Kali continues to be a fragile rabbit, but in body only. A model for my life, her attitude and spunk are humbling. She makes me laugh because she is such a *total* surprise. It wasn't that I had expected a cute, cuddly, sweet little being in the form of a rabbit. I just hadn't expected such power and strength of will. Nor had I realized she would have such a huge, albeit near silent, voice. Or such *presence.*

Methodically and repeatedly, our beautiful iron-willed maiden has destroyed every notion, every presumption, every wayward thought I ever had about rabbits.

She continues to charge into my quiet midnight times. She never asks if she can come in; she storms, barges, and breaks into my dreams. She *never* tiptoes—I don't think she knows how.

During those night visits, Kali leaps into the heavens, sprinting across the clouds, hopping from star to star—spinning, waltzing, turning, a ballet dancer of purest grace and beauty. I always follow and watch, enthralled. Then, when the moon is full, Kali leaps into the air, carrying my dreams to the heavens and gracing me with bits of wisdom and knowledge as she showers me with stardust.

ABOUT RABBITS: deafness

A rabbit adapts to deafness through the use of other senses and is highly aware of movement, shadow, and vibration. Some vibrations are more easily detected than others, depending on the material transmitting the movement. For example, vibrations coming through a wood floor are easier for a rabbit to sense than those through tile laid on cement. A hearing-impaired rabbit also comes to recognize hand signals and body language and takes cues from the behavior of his humans and other companions.

Care should be taken with activities unfamiliar to the deaf bunny, including bringing something new into the environment, as the disadvantaged rabbit will startle more readily than hearing rabbits and possibly injure himself.

Kali's Prince

Exceptional caregivers embody special qualities, including unconditional love, unending patience, and joyful acceptance. Such attributes are found not only in human helpers but in other animals as well.

This is not a story filled with tension and high drama, but rather an account of steadfast loyalty and love. It is a tale of dedication, of one small rabbit caring for his disabled mate. This devotion has been his gift to her and an inspiration to us.

I was not particularly taken with Kumar the first time I saw him. His mostly-white body with light-gray nose and ears seemed far too plain. I wasn't sure how I felt about his pink eyes either—not that I disliked pink eyes; I just was not sure.

We were at the House Rabbit Society shelter in Broomfield, Colorado—Kumar's rescue-home after he was callously dumped alongside a busy Denver highway.

His eyes begged for consideration. Although I agreed we should adopt him, I harbored the sentiment that he was not good enough for our precious little deaf rabbit, Kali. He didn't fit my image of a handsome, elegant rabbit, my choice of companion for our beautiful, black, lop-eared darling.

My husband took a more thoughtful approach. Noting Kumar's sweet temperament, John reminded me that we needed a gentle rabbit to be Kali's friend, one who wasn't too rambunctious for her slight build and fragile constitution.

We had read about the process of bonding rabbits and how discriminating, or even difficult, some bunnies can be about new friends, so John and I were grateful that someone else would oversee the process for us. If the initial meeting went well, we would leave Kali at the shelter for a few days, until she and Kumar were good friends.

Bill Reed Photography

We watched as the two neutered rabbits were put into an area specially set up for pairing. Kali became immediately terrified at the sight of a new rabbit. She stumbled to the gate, frantically beseeching me to take her out of the pen.

I can't leave her in there. She might get hurt. She's scared and needs me. I wanted to pick Kali up and hold her close. I wanted to take her home.

But then I noticed Kumar, who had retreated to the hay box and now sat quietly, munching and watching Kali, waiting for her to relax in his presence. I wondered what he sensed about her.

Give him a chance.

I had read about the highly social nature of rabbits and felt that having a special friend would benefit Kali. Give *him a chance.* The words competed with my fears.

John and I continued to observe, and within a few hours Kumar had worked his way closer to Kali. A gentle closeness, just enough to let her know she was safe with him. She was definitely cautious, but there was a slight change in her demeanor: she was beginning to relax. We decided to leave her after receiving the promise that the pair would be closely monitored, Kali would not be injured, and we would be kept apprised of the couple's progress. Trepidation accompanied me home, but I knew Kali was in capable hands.

For the first two days, there was little to report, which made me kind of nervous. But on the third day, the two rabbits were sitting together, eating hay. The next day, Kali let Kumar groom her, and the following evening we happily welcomed them home.

It was immediately obvious that Kumar adored Kali. He groomed her, offered himself as a resting place for her head when she tired of holding herself up, and shielded her body with his whenever he heard an unfamiliar sound.

He was also extravagantly theatrical—his movements so wildly exaggerated that it seemed he would injure himself. We worried something was dreadfully wrong with him, but after careful observation we recognized that he had become intentionally dramatic. Unable to discern the dangerous from the mundane in his new and unfamiliar surroundings, Kumar warned his deaf mate of every potential danger. He would also amplify his motions when Kali's third eyelids were especially troublesome and prevented clear sight. Or Kumar would thump. Powerful, resonating thumps that alerted Kali—through floor vibrations to her sensitive feet—that something was wrong.

A few days after he came to live with us, the little guy nearly had a heart attack when I brought a laundry basket upstairs. Kumar had seen me ascend and descend the stairs numerous times, but one look at that strange-looking thing in my arms resulted in his taking flying leaps across the floor and into the condo. He bounded to the top platform and, careful not to put his weight on her, placed his body protectively over Kali's.

In that instant I realized what a perfect companion Kumar was. In my mind, he was transformed from a rather plain rabbit to the most incredible, handsome, noble rabbit in the world—the ideal match for Kali. And perfectly named—Kumar, meaning *prince.*

My affection and concern for her now extended also to him. He was reacting to everything for Kali's sake, and I wondered how the stress of being constantly on alert would affect him.

To make Kumar's life easier, John and I refrained from unnecessarily alarming our tender-hearted but skittish rabbit. We watched his pink eyes, so marvelously expressive, for signs that he was worried or afraid. "Kumar, it's all right" became our stock phrase, repeated so often that he began looking at us for the reassuring words.

Even though we guarded him against anxiety and distress, he did not have a leisurely life. *I must protect my ladylove and our home* seemed to be his dictum. The sweet, gentle white bunny had his paws full trying to fulfill that promise to Kali, whose frail body belied her strong will. She didn't make it easy for him.

Kali was stalwart, unperturbed in the presence of a stranger working on a window or when a new stray cat took up residence. When we adopted a sweet-tempered dog, whose head was larger than Kali's body, she insisted on crawling over John's legs to greet the part of the prone dog that was at her level—his nose. When I came home on a pair of crutches, Kali disregarded Kumar's warning thumps, hopped over, and took a chunk out of the offensive intruders.

It took months for Kumar to relax enough to let Kali explore on her own. Even then, his eyes never lost their troubled look until she returned to his side.

Bill Reed Photography

Though he remained insecure about Kali's unexpected forays, he actively shared her dislikes. It soon became apparent that a second motto governed his life: *If she likes something, I like it; if she doesn't, neither do I.* When Kali became incensed because I put toys in their condo, Kumar threw them out. I returned them, thinking he might be playing. Kumar then, very deliberately, carried them to the stairs and violently pitched them to the landing below. His message was clear: the toys were not to appear in their condo again!

Besides being Kali's protector and champion, he was her teacher, showing her how to drink from a bowl, demonstrating how to properly groom, and sharing the delight of tasting unsweetened papaya treats. When she was not feeling well or was too tired, he would groom her completely and then offer his body as her bolster.

When Kali became critically ill, Kumar was so distraught that he stopped eating and drinking and quietly lay down beside her, seemingly ready to die with her. I syringe-fed and hydrated him until it became apparent Kali would recover. Then he became exuberant in his joy: running, hopping, spinning, and performing acrobatic feats—enough for both of them.

On days when Kali's body is not working as she would like or when she is frustrated or angry with something that limits her, Kumar is there: tender and patient, watchful and companionable, with a soft touch and encouraging nudge.

The rabbit who once was a lonely, scared castaway has found his calling: he is Kali's handsome, gracious, and perfect prince.

ABOUT RABBITS: prey animals

Rabbits' actions are greatly influenced by their prey psychology. Everything unfamiliar holds potential danger, making bunnies naturally cautious and distrustful until they verify that conditions are safe. When scared, rabbits may become aggressive in an attempt to defend themselves against perceived perils. Or they can literally become paralyzed with fear or die of fright.

To minimize a rabbit's stress, it's helpful for human guardians to understand what it means to think like a prey animal. Imagine how terrified and stressed you'd be if pursued in a strange environment, unable to find a safe place to hide, and panicked at every unfamiliar movement and sound.

Envision yourself in your rabbit's place, at her eye level. Things that are commonplace to you as a human will take on a different look and meaning, and it will be easier to discern what might frighten her.

Lovable Bobka

Information for this story was provided by Lena Sullivan

It was oppressively hot and bone dry the day someone brought five-month-old Bobka to Bryce Canyon National Park—and left him there.

One can only imagine the young rabbit's fear: no food, no water, nowhere to hide. He was all alone, except for the alarming sounds, unfamiliar odors, and hungry predators.

Domestic rabbits *cannot* survive in the wild. Fortunately for the innocent bunny, campers spotted him and never gave up as he cut back and forth, diving low and jumping high, evading capture until a lucky move snared him. A kind lady contacted Best Friends Animal Society, and the dark-brown bunny was taken to the Utah sanctuary.

There Lena met the lovable rabbit, although he was anything but sweet during their first encounter. It occurred when Bobka was being introduced to another bunny. Staff members hoped the two would become buddies, but Bobka wanted nothing to do with the other rabbit and immediately went on the offensive.

Lena admits she forgot all her training and acted impulsively: in an attempt to stop Bobka's attack, she stuck her hand between the two adversaries. Bobka bit her. *Hard!*

She assumed the bite would not be serious, but Lena soon lost all feeling in two fingers. After a trip to the emergency room and days without full use of her hand, she emerged with a new respect for an angry rabbit. And a clear understanding of why she'd been told never to stick a hand between two fighters.

The next encounter with Bobka was different—he was adorable. His charming and entertaining ways were impossible to ignore, and when Lena later moved back to her home and family in New England, the rabbit who had captured her heart went along.

Bobka treated the cross-country trip as an adventure, settled contentedly into his new life, and finished growing to the size he is today: nineteen pounds of sleek muscle, coupled with a personality that is much, much larger!

Lena delights in recounting some of the intricacies of Bobka's personality.

BOBKA IS INVENTIVE AND CLEVER.

Using his boundless imagination, Bobka often entices Lena to participate in his plans. Like the day he would not come out of his two-story condo.

Worried that he might be ill, Lena opened the doors and knelt on the floor, trying to coax him out. All of a sudden, his big black-brown body vaulted past her head and onto her back!

He dug his toes into Lena's sweatshirt and nudged her neck with his nose. She didn't budge. Bobka prompted again, tickling her cheek with his long funnel ears. Lena crawled across the room, carrying him piggyback all the way to the carpeted area. Once there, Bobka, in one fluid motion, elegantly deposited himself on the floor.

Now, whenever the four-legged jockey wants to be transported in style, he signals Lena by standing up on his hind feet and looking at her with a beatific expression, then putting his forepaws on her legs and bumping his nose against her knee.

Lena generally complies with Bobka's wishes because she loves the reward he so generously bestows: soft kisses with his warm tongue.

BOBKA IS FUN-LOVING AND MISCHIEVOUS.

His favorite furry housemate is Kip, a Pomeranian dog. When Lena adopted Bobka, she was concerned Kip might meddle with the young rabbit. Instead, the two became best friends and often follow in each other's footsteps, checking to see what the other is doing.

When Bobka wants to stir things up, he grabs one of Kip's squeaky toys, then dashes around him, inviting the dog to chase. Kip tries his hardest to keep up with the muscular, long-legged rabbit, but Bobka's air-spins and leaping turns leave the poor dog bewildered.

Kip retaliates by grabbing one of Bobka's favorite chew toys and racing in the opposite direction. A tug-of-war ensues, with low grunts and play growls adding to the theatrics.

When it's all over, the pals snuggle into Kip's bed for a nap.

BOBKA IS SHREWD AND HARD-BARGAINING.

The morning after a long day at the office, Lena always hopes for a few extra minutes of sleep. But as soon as her husband, Casey, opens the rabbit condo, Bobka charges into the bedroom, jumps onto the bed and hops all over her: his way of reminding "mom" to get up and feed him.

Of course, the jolt from his heavy body wakes Lena immediately. She sleepily caresses the dark fur on his mandolin-shaped body, and that's all it takes for Bobka to show his affection—for a second. He licks her cheek with his smooth tongue, then nestles close—and nips her chin! *It's time to feed me!*

He always makes it up to her, though. After eating his portion of pellets and vegetables, Bobka affectionately licks her hand.

BOBKA IS INDEPENDENT AND UNCONVENTIONAL.

He redefines the idea of normal rabbit conduct when he lounges on a cat perch in the window. Lying on his back, all four of his enormous paws dangling above him, Bobka enjoys the sun's warmth on his tummy.

Lena remembers how scared she was the first time she saw Bobka in that position. She quickly walked over to make sure he was breathing and gently felt his side.

Bobka flipped over, glared at her, and thumped his hind feet indignantly. As a clear indication of his displeasure, he turned his back to her before hopping off to find another sunny spot!

BOBKA IS CONFIDENT AND EXUBERANT.

He believes he is King of the House and acts the part. When he's feeling particularly majestic, Bobka pulls the large, ruby-red pillow from Lena and Casey's bedroom to the center of the living room. He settles on top of his throne and defies Kip or the family cat to challenge his sovereignty.

Other times, Bobka performs aerobatics, proclaiming his zest for life. In his unique and infectious rabbit way, he shouts to the world, "*I* am having a *VERY FINE* day!"

BOBKA IS INTELLIGENT AND IRRESISTIBLE.

As soon as they arrived in New England, Lena instituted a training program and, for the most part, her charming rabbit complied. Litter training was accomplished without a hitch. He always darts to her side when he hears his name, and "Bobka, bedtime" triggers him to run laps around the room, then hop into his house without hesitation.

In other aspects of daily living, however, Lena has had to rely on creativity and consistency because, as all rabbit-people know, rabbits like to be in charge. Bobka is an exceptionally strong-willed bunny; it's a challenge for Lena to keep him mentally stimulated so that he doesn't dig in corners or rearrange furniture.

In his artful fashion, Bobka guides his human companions. When they want to redirect his actions, he redirects theirs. Dragging his dark-blue baby blanket along, he invites them to play his version of hide-and-seek. They loosely turban him in the cotton covering; Bobka nudges his way out, grabs the blanket with his teeth, and races around the room. Then he returns to them, asking for a repeat of the game. And then, a threepeat! He's such a comic that they enjoy playing almost as much as he does.

Bobka is clever, unconventional, entertaining, irresistible, and more: he's one *lovable* rabbit!

ABOUT RABBITS: litter box training

Rabbits are most reliably litter box trained when they are spayed or neutered. They basically train themselves, though there are important considerations, such as the health of the bunny and the litter box's material, location, and roominess. The number of rabbits in the household as well as the attitude of the human caregiver will also affect a rabbit's behavior. Punishment for "mistakes" is neither warranted nor effective.

It is easiest for a bunny to become litter-trained after the age of six months, but—like young humans—they sometimes forget and must be gently reminded and occasionally assisted in their learning.

Note: Information on litter box training is readily available from rabbit rescue organizations and other sources, including a chapter in Marinell Harriman's House Rabbit Handbook.

Emily

by Susan Chernak McElroy

Her name was Emily, and I don't have a single photo of her anywhere. I do have an ornament in her honor, however. It's a blown-out eggshell that I painted in her image and on the back it reads *Emily Rabbit.* She came into my life at a blustery time, when the ground around me was uncertain and slippery. I was recuperating from cancer treatments, staying with my boyfriend, wondering where—or if—I would be the coming year.

When in a severe crisis, it has always been my habit to seek out the attention and company of animals. I find myself visiting pet stores and the local humane societies more often when life is storming around me. Sometimes I bring a new animal companion home, unconsciously hoping that a new face in the family will take some of my focus off the hurricanes in my life. It always does. Still, I would not recommend this as a sound strategy for stress reduction and life management. A new animal in the family always comes with surprises of its own. This was certainly true in the case of Emily.

I first began musing about the idea of a house rabbit when I came across the *House Rabbit Handbook* in my local pet store. A house rabbit! What a thought! And so my search began. Mike, my boyfriend, was not opposed to the notion of a rabbit in the house, as he had a special fondness in his heart for bunnies or, that is, for his own personal illusions about bunnies. Culturally, we all share some of these same rabbit fantasies: dreamy notions about the cuddliness of rabbits, their gentleness, their innocence and harmlessness. Rabbits elicit baby talk from humans, and sighs, and all thoughts wonderful and spring-like. When I updated Mike daily on my hunt for the right rabbit, he would smile fondly and his eyes would go all soft.

Down a country road not far from us lived a woman who bred mini lops, and she had a number of baby bunnies all set to go. The one I chose was a tiny female, cinnamon brown with white spots. Only five weeks old, she fit in the palm of my hand and felt as fragile as a newborn chick. We brought her home to a roomy pen set up in the living room, with a sign over it that proclaimed, "Rabbit Crossing." Mike was as fussy as a new father, fretting over whether the house was too warm for her, or too cold—or too lonely. He insisted I put a stuffed animal toy in the cage, which she promptly nibbled to shreds and made into a bed. My cat, Sushi, set up a post near Emily's pen, thrilled at this live television show that broadcast nonstop.

I pulled my scattered attention off the radiation treatments I was having each day, the doctor's appointments I attended each week, and the apprehensions of family and friends (not to mention my own) and placed it on the soothing comfort of Emily's tiny and inquisitive face. Why think of cancer when I could just look at that wiggly nose? Why wonder what turn my little lifeboat would take when I had more pleasing things to worry about, like how to housetrain a baby rabbit and how to create harmony between her and the cat?

Emily settled in easily with us. She was quiet, hungry, curious, and quite brave for her small size. She didn't shrink away when I cupped my hands around her, but she would give a fierce little kick if I did not hold her just right. The litter box in her pen was a source of wonder for her, and she would spend considerable time just sitting in it, reflecting, with her eyes half shut. Sometimes—hallelujah!—she would put it to its intended use. Within two weeks, she was bouncing confidently around the living room while we supervised. I loved it when she raced across the rug and leaped straight up, changing directions high in midair. When she landed after one of those acrobatic feats, she looked downright smug. During Emily's play sessions, Sushi was put into the back bedroom or let outside. In Mike's mind, Sushi did not look at Emily as a potential playmate but as a moving feast. I knew differently. I don't know how I knew, but I just did.

When Mike was at work one day, I introduced cat to rabbit, and they got along instantly and famously. That night when Mike got home, I took Emily out of her pen and confidently placed her on the floor next to Sushi.

Mike was horrified. "Don't do that! Cats are predators!"

As if Mike were a stage director, Sushi suddenly crouched and began stalking Emily as the rabbit bounced across the carpet, oblivious to what lurked behind her.

"Pick her up! The cat's going to eat her!"

I didn't react. They'd been doing this all day.

Emily hopped behind the kitchen counter, Sushi tight on her tail. Mike hollered, "Susan! *DO* something!" In the next instant, Sushi raced out from behind the counter with Emily hot on her tail.

This was the first time Mike had seen the other face of rabbits—the charging bunny, with mouth open and back feet thumping. Emily streaked across the carpet, leaping like a greyhound after Sushi. When she had the cat treed on top of the television, Emily stopped to lick her bunny tail and readjust her nose whiskers. After a final sonorous thump, she calmly hopped to her pen.

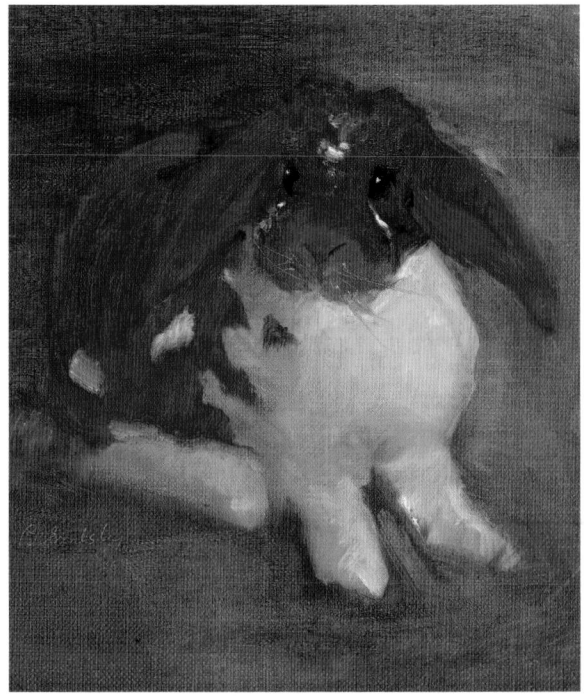

This is the nature I came to associate most deeply with Emily. Yes, of course she was sweet and floppy-eared and terminally cute, but I honestly believe her soul was that of a warrior. From her babyhood, she never suffered fools lightly, myself included. Mike had to adjust his worldview of bunny behavior fast, because after the night she ran Sushi out of the kitchen, Emily pretty much came into her own—and "her own" was the stance of a proud and impatient princess. Sushi was the first to learn of Emily's warrior-princess tendencies, but we would all learn soon enough. Just as Emily was clearly a match for Sushi, in her way she was an equal match for us.

The cat-and-rabbit chase scenes became part of family life, sometimes with Sushi as stalker, sometimes Sushi as prey. Other scenarios were enacted between Emily and me. Sometimes I'd lift her away from chewing on a table leg and she would lie passively in my arms; other times she'd charge my ankles when I tried to distract her from dismantling something I treasured. Her charges were always accompanied by a nasty little growl, and she'd stamp her foot to make her point absolutely certain. If that didn't work, she'd escalate by shaking her ears from side to side while growling and thumping. Mike would never venture near her at moments like this. Any time she got belligerent, her family status changed from *our* rabbit to *my* rabbit.

I never thought of her as cranky. In my eyes, Emily was all the things I wanted to be at that time in my life: strong, self-confident, genuine, direct, honest, sure of personal boundaries. She also had her soft, contemplative side—moments when she delighted in snuggling on my lap or nibbling a grape leaf out in the yard, her eyes all faraway and her jaw munching in a kind of earnest concentration. When she felt like it, she would come when called and race to our feet quick as a flash. She understood "no" and would respect it, but usually accompanied her compliance with a growl. At the time, I was reading books by Dr. Bernie Siegel about cancer survivorship—survivors generally being those who are not docile patients. Emily wasn't docile about anything, but neither was she offensive in her assertiveness. I saw her as a symbol of life—lived with vitality and on one's own terms—and I loved her for it.

Before Emily was a year old, I noticed a funny lump forming on the back of her shoulders, just behind her ears. Our veterinarian recommended surgery and—in accordance with the instructions in my rabbit care books—I asked the vet if she was knowledgeable about the needs of rabbits. She assured me she was, and so I sent Emily off for her surgery with confidence. The operation went fine, the tumor was benign, and I sighed with relief. Emily would not face the kind of exhaustive treatments that had loomed in front of me for so long.

But two days after surgery, things went wrong.

I'd been giving Emily a liquid antibiotic that the vet had assured me was safe for rabbits' delicate digestive systems. It was not. I woke up one morning to a listless bunny covered in murky liquid: her droppings, turned to the consistency of water. Her appetite was gone, her ability to hop gone with it, and she had a horrid, dull look in her eyes. Even her soft fur suddenly felt greasy and smelled sour. I was on the phone to the vet instantly. Emily's health had gone from just-great to critical in thirty-six hours.

The next few days went by in a crazy blur, so reminiscent of my own health fears that I could scarcely breathe into the next moment. Of course, there was medicine to be given my poor, very sick rabbit, along with probiotics to support her digestive system. The hardest treatment for both of us to endure, however, was the insertion of the IV needle under her skin, necessary for the frequent saline drips to keep her hydrated and to avoid kidney failure.

Emily was a good patient. She accepted all my clumsy attempts at nursing with passivity and silence. Forcing medicine and probiotics into her small mouth and piercing her clay-like skin with needles generated no resistance from her. She lay inert on the dining room table—IV bag hanging from the chandelier, tube trailing to her shoulders—staring quietly at nothing.

Suddenly, I understood down to my bones what Dr. Siegel had meant when he wrote that survivors were not necessarily "good" patients. Life should be infused with fervor and spunk, qualities that Emily had seemingly lost. All the traits that made caring for her so *easy*—her listlessness, her quietness, the utter disengagement with her surroundings—felt ominous and deadly. As I tended her, my hands sought vitality and a spark of animation, but found only docility and resignation. And that terrified me.

Time passed, and the days all ran together. Emily was still alive. I swaddled her in terry cloth and diapers between treatments in an attempt to keep her clean and dry. Sometimes when I held her, she would shiver and lick my hand. She was such a good patient—until the moment when she was not. I had lifted her up to the dining room table for her injection and felt her body tense. She wiggled in my hands. I tightened my grip, surprised. For a number of days, she'd been hanging from my fingers like a rag. Now, with one hand steadying her, I reached for a needle and popped off the protective cover. She sat quietly until I eased the needle under the skin along her nape. With a grunt, she whirled her head around and glared at me. Then she uttered the sound that made me realize she would be just fine: Emily growled.

Although I'd successfully doctored her by myself for several days, those days were over. I had to wait until Mike came home from work because it now took four hands (preferably five) to give her the medicine and the injections. She wasn't nasty about any of it, just resolute and disgusted and willing to let us know it. Two days later, Emily was charging after Sushi and giving threatening looks at my ankles when I scooted her away from the table legs. So happy was I to see and feel the robust life pouring back into her that I would've been delighted to sacrifice one of my toes to her blustery indignation.

Emily had many more opportunities in her life to be a patient: the tumor returned now and again, one of her teeth came out and the opposing one needed to be trimmed regularly, and she lost a toenail in a mishap. But she was never again a *patient* patient. She was a warrior survivor, and she showed me how to become one as well. I never growled at anyone, nor bit an ankle, but I did become free of cancer. And I send a prayer of remembrance and gratitude to the fierce bunny who taught me how.

ABOUT RABBITS: their true nature

Baby bunnies are definitely adorable, but they do grow up! When they enter adolescence (at approximately 3-1/2 months of age), the once-amiable bunnies begin to display a strong will, a desire for autonomy, and the innate desire to chew and dig.

Not only do rabbits "speak" through a repertoire of sounds and body language, but they may also convey their fears and dislikes by nipping or even biting. Their human guardians should not punish or yell at the bunny for such actions but instead should take the time to learn and appreciate what the bunny is trying to communicate.

As prey animals, rabbits depend on their intelligence and good memories, and they display characteristics (such as being wily and inventive) that make them amusing—and sometimes challenging—companions. They are highly social creatures, which explains the displays of affection and charm for which rabbits are known and loved; it also explains their need for companionship and regular interaction.

Note: Reference the article, "Veterinary Care: Rabbit Basics," at the back of the book for information on some of the medications toxic to rabbits.

A Real Head-Turner

Information for this story was provided by Patrice Pruitte

He was an unwanted, backyard hutch rabbit. Except for visits by menacing predators and ruffians and by a human who sporadically delivered food and water, the domestic, long-haired bunny lived in solitary confinement. The outdoor hutch was falling in on itself. The rabbit lived in terror, but not for much longer—the predators were making inroads.

A neighbor felt sorry for the little bunny and snuck food to him when she could. She noticed that the child for whom the rabbit had been purchased never played with or cared for him.

Finally, the woman could stand it no longer; her heart filled with mercy, she called a friend, who called her sister. . . .

And that is how I heard about the fuzzy lop who desperately needed a new home.

I did not want to take him in. Our beloved brown-and-white Dutch rabbit, Chance, was ailing and needed me. But options were nonexistent: as an active volunteer, I knew there wasn't room at the Rabbit Sanctuary; no one I knew was able to take another rabbit on such short notice; and, if he remained in his current situation, the bunny would not live much longer.

My husband made it easy; he brought the bunny home.

"You won't believe how much fur this rabbit has. Or how matted it is!" Ronnie exclaimed as he entered the house.

I looked inside the small carrier and saw a shaggy animal with a large round head and flat face. Not very rabbit-like, I thought, but cute.

As I watched, the begrimed, tangled mess of a rabbit slowly turned his head from side to side, in a never-ending motion: back and forth, back and forth. The movement was very different from the normal scanning done by rabbits to help reference the objects around them.

"He did that all the way home," Ronnie said in response to my questioning look.

When I reached into the carrier to retrieve our new family member, his fright was obvious: bugged eyes; rapid, almost spastic, breathing; shudders and twitches as if he were on the verge of a seizure.

We carefully placed him in our screened porch, near an open bunny condo. We left the door from the porch to the house open too, so he could roam far and wide, but the frightened little guy immediately chose the security of the condo.

We stayed and watched him settle in. That's when we decided to name him Buffalo because, in profile, his large head, shoulders hunched in stress, and shaggy coat made him look like a diminutive version of his namesake.

Days later, I was fretting about the incessant head-turning, his refusal to come out of his rabbit shelter, the fact that he preferred hiding to eating.

I was also frantic about balancing the care Buffalo needed with all that Chance required.

"It's not that I don't want to spend time with you, but I need to be with Chance too. She's old, and she won't live much longer." My voice cracked as I talked about our precious Dutch rabbit.

It was obvious Buffalo had been psychologically traumatized, but I had no idea how to penetrate his emotional morass. His eyes, the dull deep red of unpolished garnet, had a vacant, unfocused look. I feared the sensitive waif would die.

"Please, help me to help you," I pleaded.

Next thing I knew, I was trying to reason with him, telling him he had to do his part and trust us. My words just tumbled out. I argued against his death; I cajoled, bargained, begged.

The next morning, Buffalo ate all his pellets.

The following afternoon, he came out of his roomy condo. He immediately took up residence out of sight behind a swivel rocker, but I was heartened. It was progress.

"Good for you, sweet boy," I murmured as he snatched a piece of romaine lettuce from my hand.

When Buffalo began exploring the porch, it was with a slow creeping movement, never a hop.

Insecure and frightened, he always sought refuge at the slightest sound or movement. Unnaturally cautious and lacking curiosity—he just wasn't acting like a rabbit.

Buffalo consistently avoided entering the house. One day we carried him in, and he immediately panicked. We had to return him to the porch, his safe haven. I cradled his sides with my palms and held him on my lap, trying to arrest the violent quakes that seemed to overtake his three-pound body. He crouched down, trying to make himself smaller. His head was turning back and forth, back and forth.

"It's all right, sweet one."

But it wasn't, and I wondered: *Will your emotional scars ever heal? Will you ever be free of your horrible dread?*

I felt I was failing Buffalo, but I didn't know what to do. The head-turning remained a mystery. Perhaps it provided comfort, much like a disturbed child rocking himself. Or maybe the movement was an escape mechanism, a way to shut out the world when it became too scary. No one I spoke with could offer a valid explanation, only that the stress Buffalo had endured the first two years of his life had profoundly affected him. Be patient, they advised.

Sensitive to Buffalo's emotional needs, Ronnie and I spent time with the bunny on his turf. We sat in the screened porch and tried to tempt him with toys, petted him when he would come within reach, and removed a mat or two from his silky coat whenever possible. I started reading to him from my collection of children's storybooks about rabbits. We gave him time, and more time.

"With love and the right environment, rabbits can overcome adverse beginnings," I kept telling myself.

The holiday season came, a time of mourning the loss of our sweet Chance. Our only decoration was a tiny tree with rabbit ornaments. A vigil light shone through the window onto her fresh grave.

The New Year began on a brighter note: Buffalo began to relax with our handling. We managed to snip off the remainder of the mats and gently loosen tangles; his varicolored Angora coat began to transform into the beautiful covering it was meant to be. After each grooming session, we brought him just inside the door, hoping the close proximity to the porch would allay some of his anxiety. But, alas, he planted his stocky back feet in place and remained motionless, clearly afraid.

Seven months passed. One day Buffalo came to the door and, amazingly, took a step inside the house. He sat there, uncertain, and then retreated. But it was a breakthrough.

Then, on a particularly cold morning in May, I closed the door to the porch, only to hear scratching a few minutes later.

I opened the door, in time to see Buffalo dash into hiding. I left it open, and our fuzzy lop ventured in! Not very far, not for very long, but he came into the house on his own. My hopes soared.

Ronnie and I marked time by Buffalo's forays into the unknown. Fourteen months after coming to our house, he took a short nap on the plush carpet in the living room.

On the anniversary of Chance's death, Buffalo slept in the den, closer to our bedroom. A week later, he started

running and hopping! Then, miraculously, the head-turning behavior disappeared.

That Christmas, the unfamiliar sight of our large evergreen tree sent Buffalo back into the grip of terror. We held him and loved him, but for two weeks the porch was his asylum.

The morning Buffalo rejoined us, he raced past the tree and into the den. He peeked around the door and then courageously positioned himself to watch the towering, needle-leafed intruder. Later that day, searching for him, I discovered Buffalo soundly asleep—under the Christmas tree!

I laughed and I cried. Our little Buffalo was healing.

Then came a day I will always remember: Valentine's Day, and Buffalo sought *me* out. His intense garnet-colored eyes, clear and sparkling with mischief, said, "Play with me!" And that wasn't all; he actually began asking Ronnie for back rubs.

Buffalo was transforming, day by day. He eagerly explored the house, hid under beds and in cardboard boxes, and discovered the versatility of phone books. Exhibiting the wonderful disposition of a happy rabbit, he saw everything as an adventure.

Today Buffalo is a gorgeous rabbit. When he moves, his fur is an undulating wave of beige, misty gray, and white. If lying in repose, his white throat and belly shimmer in the light. He hops, and his dark gray ears flop in graceful rhythm. When asking for a treat, he displays delicate front paws—one white, one gray.

It took more than two years, but Buffalo finally knows he is safe and in his forever home. Now, he runs to greet us, his eyes bright and knowing, and we see a rabbit who comprehends love. He runs to greet others and always receives a second glance, and a third. Buffalo is so handsome, and he exudes such happiness and personality. The once traumatized and fearful rabbit is a beautiful example of confidence, sweetness, and charm—he's become a *real* head-turner!

ABOUT RABBITS: backyard hutches

Rabbits who live in outdoor hutches receive virtually no mental stimulation and little protection. Predators are able to access many hutches, chewing or tearing them apart. Even if an enclosure is inaccessible, the mere presence of a predator can cause a rabbit to panic and injure herself or to go into shock and die.

Most hutches provide limited refuge from wind, freezing temperatures, heat, rain, and snow. In addition, nearly all hutches are too small and most have wire floors—a combination that leads to obesity, weak muscles, deformed spines, damaged feet, and other health problems. Poor husbandry and the lack of adequate health care result in many preventable maladies.

The fact that backyard hutch rabbits generally live alone and receive limited human interaction prevents their lively and intricate natures from developing fully. Domestic rabbits are the third most popular mammalian pet, underscoring their initial appeal as companions. But they are also the most likely to be abandoned or taken to an animal shelter (where they are likely to be euthanized).

Humans must be emotionally involved with their rabbits in order to have happy, healthy pets—and backyard hutch rabbits are too often denied that emotional commitment.

Three Stately Ladies, One Noble Baron

"It's not a matter of *if*, but *when*."

For weeks the words had been my daily mantra, but today I was having a hard time believing them. My quest to bond four rabbits into a group had been, thus far, wildly unsuccessful. Baron, a gentle soul, was the only male in the group. The three females—Bailey, Majesty, and Spirit—were each determined to be the dominant rabbit. Again and again, I'd had to intervene and separate the trio.

Bailey was deaf. She was also filled with determination, tenacity, and resourceful intelligence. Brimming with confidence, the caramel-colored, five-pound mini lop *knew* it was her birthright to roam throughout the house at any time. To her mind, the entire house was her territory.

Majesty had grown in stature and poise after her near-miss with death. Her former family had tired of having rabbits and quit caring for them; she was the lone survivor. The majestic black rabbit, initially distrustful of humans and fearful of being touched, was now self-assured and no longer hesitated to assert her strength.

Spirit was energy incarnate! She was fortunate to have been found in an empty house after her people had moved. The ruby-eyed Himalayan was willful, agile, and faster than any rabbit in the house. Spirit's nerve and strength of character more than made up for her small build.

The three females had one common denominator: each was a sweet-tempered rabbit. I was learning, however, that this sweetness did not extend to one another. They saved all their affection for Baron, the good-natured, charcoal-colored satin male.

I hadn't thought that establishing the little warren would be so difficult. I worked from home, which simplified the frequent supervision that bonding can require. I already knew it was a matter of time and patience, though my previous experiences with forming rabbit groups had generally been accomplished within a week or two. In addition, I knew that Bailey was the dominant rabbit, and I assumed that Majesty and Spirit would rather quickly acknowledge that fact as well.

Valerie Fox

How very wrong I was! My naiveté made me no match for the rabbits.

The bonding pen, set in a neutral area, contained get-away spots: a cardboard tube and two boxes with holes cut in the sides. I wanted the smaller rabbits to have escape routes if a larger one became over-energetic or combative.

Days one through four had passed quietly. Bailey and Baron, long-time mates, seemed more than willing to share space with Majesty and Spirit. The four ate together and, though they did not snuggle, they also did not fight. Baron exhibited his natural love for Bailey's company and, always congenial, established a friendly pattern with the other two females as well.

Early the fifth morning, Bailey had had enough of the close quarters. She tried opening the gate with her teeth; failing that, she charged the pen, knocking one side askew. Before I could get her out, Bailey whirled and struck out at Spirit, then at Majesty. The next few moments were filled with strife; I had all I could do to restrain the angry lop.

Once free of the fenced-in area, Bailey raced to the other end of the house. She gazed around the bedroom, scurried under the bed, and stretched out to relax.

Meanwhile, Majesty and Spirit seemed hell-bent on establishing dominance. I was concerned for Spirit's safety, given her petite size, but she quickly maneuvered around the boxes that were in the pen.

I came to realize that the size of the bonding area was a problem. Majesty needed a small space in order to curb her territorial tendencies. In contrast, Bailey found the enclosure too confining and would act up. I felt as though I was in a sort of shuffle game, moving the rabbits—with the necessary items such as litter boxes, hay, and water—

from small space to larger, and back again. Additional barriers were necessary at night to keep them separated but within close proximity.

The repetitive schedule stretched into weeks, each day revolving around supervision of the rabbits' time together and then providing space for their individual freedom. Bailey would always choose to go to the bedroom. Spirit, whose diminutive body fit into places the others could not access, delighted in finding what she considered secret spots. Majesty and Baron never ventured far.

Majesty had become bullish, Bailey belligerent, Spirit impudent. I was relieved that Baron continued to exhibit his noble tendencies.

But I was about ready to give up.

"It's not a matter of *if*, but *when*," I reminded myself aloud.

I thought about why I had wanted to form the group in the first place: rabbits' communal nature assists them when one becomes ill or dies. Therefore, my efforts to bond the four companions might in the future provide them great solace.

The doorbell rang, reminding me of the remodel work to be done in the hallway. Two men entered with their tools, removed a door, and began tearing out a portion of the wall.

Worried about how the noise and dust would affect the rabbits, I moved the four into the same room with my other bunnies. The rabbits appeared rather anxious, noses twitching as they tried to ascertain what was going on. Bailey's deafness, however, desensitized her to the clamor.

Sharon Barrett Kennedy

Sharon Barrett Kennedy

A loud crash resounded through the house, and the hearing rabbits immediately reacted. Majesty, upright ears flattened against her back, froze in a crouched position. Spirit, ruby-eyes dilated, wiggled between Majesty and the wall. Baron tucked himself in front of them. They huddled together, feeling safer in each other's company.

Bailey, unaffected by the racket, foraged on hay. She would take frequent breaks to snuggle close to Baron, appearing to stare defiantly at Majesty and Spirit.

She sauntered around in her confident way and, at one point, presented herself to Majesty for grooming. Majesty capitulated! I could hardly believe my eyes when she began grooming Bailey's face. After a few moments, Bailey moved and lowered her head to Spirit. Again, I was surprised at the positive response.

I wanted to shout my joy! The foursome was going to work. The day of *when* had finally arrived.

The banging and drilling in the hallway continued for hours. By the time the construction workers left, the four rabbits were snuggled close for comfort.

The days that followed were filled with challenges since the strong-willed females still had some dominance issues to work out. But the breakthrough had come.

Someday I hope Bailey, Majesty, and Spirit will be steadfast and peaceable friends. For now, it's enough that the three stately ladies have decided to get along and share time with the amiable Baron, who shares affection with them all.

ABOUT RABBITS: making friends

Rabbits can be very picky about their choice of companions. Some become friends quickly, while others require months to become close. Putting rabbits together and expecting them to immediately like each other is unrealistic and unfair. Hostility between rabbits (especially if any are unaltered) may result in serious, life-threatening fights.

Though domestic rabbits are communal creatures, the successful bonding of two or more bunnies generally requires attention, time, patience, and (ideally) a neutral space. When the friendship is cemented, it is a wonderful feeling to know that two or more convivial fur-friends have each other for comfort and camaraderie while family members engage in work, school, and other activities. An added benefit is that a companion reduces boredom and the related destructive chewing. Finally, it's a pleasure to be welcomed home by happy bunnies—and watching their antics provides delightful entertainment!

Interiors by Taz

Information for this story was provided by Elisha Bunting

Elisha was smitten the first time she saw the light-gray, pug-nosed Holland lop.

Her feelings were not returned.

Elisha offered the back of her hand for the new arrival to sniff.

Taz, his name according to the cage tag, transformed from a cute little bunny into a menacing attacker. Tail up and body tense, he lunged at her. Harsh snorts warned her away.

Elisha immediately backed up but was unfazed. She knew the small rabbit was just trying to defend himself and that he probably had good reason.

"What's his story?" she asked.

"He arrived from the clinic an hour ago," her co-worker replied, referring to the veterinary clinic where animals are taken upon arrival at Best Friends Animal Society. "He came from an elementary school."

That explained much. Elisha knew that most school classrooms are unsuitable for rabbits: the social animals too often exist in small cages, without regular exercise or adequate stimulation for their inquisitive minds. In addition, children—in their eagerness to interact with the animals—often poke objects into the cage, creating a fearful and defensive rabbit. It was likely that whoever had previously been responsible for Taz didn't understand his nature or his needs.

She peered at the lop, now immobile and flattened to the floor of his cage, as though trying to vanish from sight.

"He puts up a defense when someone gets too close, but this little guy is absolutely petrified," Elisha observed.

A look of determination fixed on her face. She would help him learn to trust again, step by step. The first phase: tidying his cage. She opened it and, as she anticipated, the terrified bunny launched himself at her.

Elisha Bunting

Using a towel as a barrier against the agitated rabbit, in record time a clean litter box and heavy water bowl were in place, the door latched.

A furious Taz reacted to Elisha's encroachment: he shredded the towel that cushioned the cage floor, flung hay about, scratched food pellets into the clutter. He studied his work and, apparently not satisfied with the mess he had created, began pushing against the water crock. It tilted, then emptied.

Half-smiling as she watched the zealous rabbit express his anger, Elisha shook her head in disbelief when the three-pound lop, small enough to easily sit on top of a paperback book, pulled the full-sized litter box to the center of the cage, got his head under it, and tip. . .*tip*. . .*TIPPED* it over.

In less than ten minutes: a shambles!

Elisha was not about to let the fast-acting bohemian sit on the damp floor; she duplicated her earlier actions, this time fastening a water bottle after removing the bowl.

The daily pattern was established. Taz became a raging, destructive fiend whenever Elisha dared intrude into his home. In turn, Elisha visibly brightened whenever she looked at the bushy-banged lop. She thought everything about him—expression, actions, and attitude—was adorable.

Learning more about Taz's early history shed light on his behavior. While in the school classroom, he had lived with another rabbit. The two neutered bunnies were bonded companions; they comforted and loved one another. One weekend they were left without adequate food and water. Taz somehow survived; his best friend did not. After that tragic event, Taz was given to one of the children, whose mother immediately noted medical problems. Not knowing how to properly care for a rabbit, she made arrangements with Best Friends and drove Taz from Arizona to the sanctuary in Utah.

At his new home, Taz sometimes vented his rage, distrust, and frustration on everyone and everything. Other times he acted so withdrawn and despondent over the loss of his dearest rabbit friend that staff members worried about his will to survive.

Elisha concentrated on befriending Taz and finding ways to pique his interest. It was a relief when, after eleven days at the Bunny House, he began showing interest in his surroundings, a sign the small lop was ready for something new.

Elisha carried his cage to an empty outdoor play area, quickly opened his door, then stepped out of the enclosure. Taz charged out, spun and looked around. Satisfied he was alone, he crouched down, using his superior hearing and smell to inspect the unfamiliar setting.

Abruptly, he jumped straight into the air. Dark eyes sparkling, Taz hopped, leaped, kicked, side-jumped. His lop ears flopped in rhythmic tempo; his movements caused the coral-hued sand to pattern around him. Taz seemed a bunny without a care in the world.

As suddenly as the frolic began, it ended. Taz sat quietly cleaning himself and then repeated the entire routine again. And again.

Elisha, jubilant to see "her" rabbit so happy, stepped inside the enclosure to play with Taz—and met his furious alter ego. Mouth open, he barreled forward, a rumbling growl in his throat.

Elisha refused to be upset. As she herded the young rabbit into his cage, she confidently promised him that some day soon he would trust her. But as soon as the door closed, Taz's eyes turned dull; his head slumped dejectedly to the floor—he hated being confined. The dramatic change in his demeanor affected the normally composed Elisha. She began crying, recognizing that Taz, in his rabbit way, was weeping too.

Weeks turned into months. One sunny autumn day, Elisha succeeded in becoming the first person to groom Taz without being bitten. The "little monster" turned into her "sweet cuddlebun." He even began grooming himself while sitting on her lap. What an amusing contrast: the "messiest rabbit ever" was singularly meticulous in his personal habits.

The New Year arrived. Elisha introduced Taz to Chaunta, rescued by a good-hearted man watering his rosebushes. The abandoned rabbit, just eight weeks old at the time, had been nearly invisible as she crouched among the thorny plants. Persistence paid off, and she was captured and taken to Best Friends.

At first, Chaunta was very displeased with the partner Elisha selected for her and launched into a tiff. Taz responded in like manner. Elisha supervised, blithely certain the strong-tempered rabbits would work out their dominance issues. They did.

Now two beautiful lop-eared rabbits—the dove-gray Taz and the charcoal-colored Chaunta—share a room specially built just for them. Taz continues to exhibit his peculiar, disheveled decorating style, while Chaunta specializes in rearranging furniture. Her favorite activity is running to other parts of the bunny-proofed house and nosing around, to her liking, items large and small. Taz willingly follows his partner everywhere and acts as her assistant.

And who lovingly watches over them? Elisha, of course. She adopted the pair and delights in seeing them exhibit the full range of their personalities. Taz frequently shows his appreciation and affection by crawling onto her lap and licking her hand before dashing off to rejoin his honeybun.

Taz and Chaunta: the two glory in their freedom, in the joy of turning everything into something fun. With Elisha's tolerant understanding and care, theirs is a world of possibilities!

ABOUT RABBITS: when a bunny's furred friend dies

When a rabbit loses a partner, it's very important he be allowed to reconcile himself to the friend's death. The bunny should be permitted to remain with the dead body in the privacy of the rabbits' home, where he may groom the body, snuggle with it, or even drag it around, trying to get his best friend to "wake up." It may take several hours, but eventually the bunny will move away from the body, realizing that his partner is gone.

If a rabbit isn't given the opportunity to come to terms with his partner's death—if the friend just disappears—he'll be bewildered, anxious, heartbroken, and perhaps angry. He may sink into a deep depression, sometimes refusing to eat or drink. Like humans and other animals, rabbits need closure when their best friends die.

A rabbit who is permitted to come to terms with his companion's death will go through a period of grieving, usually lasting two or three weeks. He will seem to be a little "down," but generally won't be so deeply depressed that he quits eating or drinking. Spend extra time with him and share his grief—he'll understand that you're hurting too. Occasionally, the bunny will need to complete the grieving process before he is comfortable meeting another potential rabbit partner. But it's not unusual for a bunny who has accepted his companion's death to break out of the grieving pattern when appropriately introduced to a new and compatible pal.

The Tilted Butterfly

Information for this story was provided by Stephen Guida

My heart fractured around the edges as I stared at her: a gnarled ball of tan-and-white fur, patched with bare skin raw from urine burn. And her head was all wrong. Fixed at a ninety-degree angle, it lay sideways and parallel to the padded-cage floor. Only one eye was visible; wide with apprehension, it pointed toward the ceiling.

Pity, anger, and powerlessness replaced my confidence. I barely heard a voice recounting the recent events: originally called in on a case of dog abuse, authorities had found the injured rabbit in a tiny, filthy wire cage in the backyard. Rescued along with the canines, she had been taken to Brambley Hedge Rabbit Rescue.

Estimated to be six months old, the lop-eared bunny had been the victim of violence. A veterinarian diagnosed neurological damage due to neck injury and perhaps permanent damage to her inner ear. The result: a severe impairment and lack of balance that destined her to a tilted view of the world.

A sudden movement startled the defenseless rabbit. Her eye filled with dread; she flinched in fear and began to panic.

And then it happened.

Losing her balance, she pitched to her side. Kicking desperately in an attempt to return to a sitting position, her frail body slammed into the walls of the padded cage. She began rolling uncontrollably; her head bobbled as it followed the fast rotation of her body, spinning, twisting, whirling.

It seemed forever before comforting hands held the rabbit upright, but the entire incident had taken just seconds. The dizziness passed and the bunny's rapid breathing slowed. She stilled, and her dark eye once more aimed skyward.

My heart sank as the full extent of her condition became apparent. Although I had agreed to be her foster-parent, I had never cared for a disabled bunny before. Questions raced through my mind: *Will you have to spend the rest of your life inside a padded cage? How will I keep you safe? Will you ever get better? What can I possibly do to help you gain some semblance of a normal life?*

Then Baby Girl, as I had already named her, shifted her head just slightly and her coffee-colored eye interrupted my thoughts. Can I trust you?

I slowly reached forward. Baby Girl allowed me to stroke her soft fur, calming further under my touch.

I'll never harm you.

Despite those true words, my concerns remained. I was afraid for her, afraid of my ignorance.

To manage those fears, I learned how to meet her most immediate needs—feeding, cleaning, and picking her up. At my first attempt, I failed to hold her properly and Baby Girl became frantic in her insecurity. I became equally frantic as she nearly squirmed out of my arms in an effort to find something solid beneath her feet.

When I finally got the knack of lifting and holding her, she trustingly leaned her worn body against me. What a thrill that was. I remember feeling Baby Girl's heart racing and thumping. Or was it mine?

I took her home, and my days developed a gentle rhythm as I became Baby Girl's parent, nurse, waiter, and guardian. I performed every routine task necessary for keeping my disabled charge fed, clean, medicated, dry, safe.

Without complaint, Baby Girl allowed me to care for her and willingly took her medications. I gently massaged her body, hoping to perhaps reverse some of the damage to her neck. In response, she'd blissfully relax and move her jaws rapidly back and forth, making a soft purring sound with her teeth. To give Baby Girl something different to look at, I began carrying her from window to window so she could see the world beyond the house—she seemed to love this, and so did I.

Baby Girl was so helpless and prone to "episodes" that I moved my home office into the living room where she was. I became nearly compulsive in my efforts to do things quietly, to refrain from any fast or unfamiliar movements that might trigger a thrashing, tumbling scare. I made mistakes, like the day I unloaded supplies in the living room. Since Baby Girl had seen the boxes, I didn't think twice when the time came to move them into the garage.

I lifted a large box. Baby Girl panicked as her skyward-looking eye spied the dark, unfamiliar form suddenly appearing in her field of vision. She teetered, flipped over, and tumbled around and around until I could open her cage and stop her.

Finally my terrified foster bunny was in my arms. Eyes bulging, heart racing, lungs sucking air, she cuddled into me and gradually relaxed as her dizziness subsided.

I'm so sorry. So very sorry. The words were an incessant parade in my mind.

She stirred and her dark eye interrupted my thoughts. I trust you.

Everything stilled. Awareness flowed through me: Baby Girl was an extraordinary gift—and she'd been given to me.

She shouldn't be captive in a cage; she deserved better than that. When I felt she had gained enough strength, Baby Girl enjoyed daily time in a playpen; gradually, she began inching slowly around it.

Stephen Guida

One spring day, I decided she was ready for something new and cleared a space in the living room. The vernal equinox was just days away and it was unseasonably warm; "Spring" from Vivaldi's *Four Seasons* graced the air, befitting the occasion.

I reached into Baby Girl's cage and picked her up, carefully supporting her backside with one hand, nestling her front paws and head against me with the other. Our usual morning meander was shortened by my impatience. A stop at one window allowed her to see the goings-on outside, and then. . . .

I carefully positioned Baby Girl on the living room carpet.

Making sure all four feet were square beneath her, my hands cradled her in place. Doubts began their harassment: *What if she loses her balance and starts spinning? What if she gets hurt?* Now that the time had come, I was loath to let go.

But Baby Girl was ready and nipped my finger to show her impatience!

Time to let go.

She excitedly looked around, her "up" eye scanning the room, her "down" eye focused on the floor. She took a couple of tentative test-steps. For thirty seconds she was in a new world. Then she slipped.

My heart slammed into my ribs. I wouldn't get to her fast enough.

Baby Girl flipped over onto her side, but instead of spinning out of control, she did a complete barrel-roll and righted herself. She regained her footing! On her own!

Utter relief flooded me. Elation surged through my veins. My chest buoyed with pride: I was like the father who saw his child take her first steps. With wonder and excitement, mixed with a huge dose of trepidation, I watched Baby Girl take baby-step after baby-step. My heart seemed to fail each time she lost balance, then started beating again when she regained her foothold.

In an effort to calm myself, I pulled the morning newspaper to the floor. I glanced at a headline, peeked at Baby

Girl, skimmed a phrase, and gave it up. I couldn't read; my only interest was this bit of bunny making her own history.

She wobbled back to me and stared me in the face, then nudged me with her white nose as if to say, Well, how about *THAT!*

I couldn't resist. I pulled her close and hugged her, my little special-needs bunny who was working so hard. Explaining that she had exercised her weak body enough for one day, I gathered her up, and we resumed our daily amble about the house.

Stephen Guida

When we stopped at Baby Girl's favorite window, monarch butterflies—those amazingly beautiful messengers of spring—fluttered about the orange trumpet-shaped flowers of the Cape May honeysuckle bushes. The sight of them capped an already perfect morning.

After that red-letter spring day, Baby Girl began roaming free when the other rabbits were in their condos.

She graduated to a slow, careful walk.

Months passed. She began scampering across the carpet. Then darting.

Not long after that, another banner day: Baby Girl ran! Admittedly it was a kind of lopsided effort as she ran in a right-turn circle, the only direction her head-tilt allowed. Then she took a flying leap of faith and landed true on her feet inside the litter box! *MY* head-tilt bunny performed a feat not normally attempted by one with such fragile balance. Her exit was not as graceful, but she made it.

Wow! Baby Girl!

That night the padded cage took up permanent residence in the garage, and Baby Girl gained her own rabbit condo.

A confident, sparkly-eyed Baby Girl began asserting herself, zigzagging swiftly away when she didn't want to be picked up. She greeted each day with enthusiasm; I marveled at her transformation.

Spring came 'round again, and it was time for another new experience. I decided to let Baby Girl meet Cisco, a large, handsome satin-mix who was my unfailing "nurse bunny." He bounded over to Baby Girl. She stopped dead in her tracks, her amazement at this living, breathing, bouncing ball of black fur almost palpable.

Cisco bowed his head to the floor, asking to be groomed. Baby Girl would do no such thing! She joyfully ran all around him, nudging and sniffing, then shoved her head underneath his, insisting he groom her instead. Gentle soul that he is, Cisco initiated grooming, and the two of them happily exchanged affection.

When she tired, Baby Girl draped herself over Cisco's recumbent body, using him as a big warm pillow. He recognized she was special and seemed to enjoy supporting her delicate body.

Later that morning, Baby Girl and I took our daily stroll through the house. Vivaldi's masterpiece was a murmur in the background as I walked to the window so she could view her favorite honeysuckle bush. My heralds of spring were back: large monarchs decorated the flowered shrub with their gorgeous orange-and-black wings.

One of the beauties sailed toward the honeysuckle, its wings held in a V. I wanted to see it through Baby Girl's eyes and mimicked her head position.

The butterfly tilted. I saw the delicate tremors of the lacy wing, the tan underside, the sun's rays piercing the shimmering black veins and tiny white spots in the black borders. I was seeing what Baby Girl saw. We were experiencing together the exquisite beauty of the monarch, the pure simplicity of the moment.

And then it happened.

My notions about Baby Girl being different, about her being a disabled bunny, took wing and floated away. Everything seemed to spin around the awareness that Baby Girl was a normal bunny.

My perceptions, my definitions, my labels—they had precluded me from seeing her as she really was. Oh, sure, I rarely noticed the head tilt anymore, but Baby Girl had always been my "special needs" bunny.

Now I knew better. But she hadn't changed, I *had.*

I get it. BABY GIRL, I GET IT!

Her self-possessed nature shone through her bright eye as she steadily looked into mine.

Yes. Given enough time, I knew you would.

ABOUT RABBITS: a bunny's body—and handling

A rabbit's body is composed of a well-developed musculature, especially in the hindquarters. The rabbit's muscles encompass a disproportionately greater mass than the delicate skeleton. This muscle-to-bone ratio underscores the necessity for exercise and playtime. Confinement and lack of exercise result in frail bones (osteoporosis) and weak muscles, which make the rabbit susceptible to injuries, some of them life-threatening.

Injuries also result from improper handling and can include fracture of the vertebrae and damage to the bunny's spinal cord. Being dropped or forced to jump from too high a place is likely to damage legs and leg joints. The number of rabbits injured and disabled by improper handling is one of the reasons rabbit-knowledgeable people declare that bunnies are not good pets for young children.

Frankie's Foible

by Nancy LaRoche

Information for this story was provided by Bea LeNoir

The black-and-white rabbit crouched in a carrier on the seat of the patrol car, ears pricked forward as the patrolwoman and a gruff voice talked on the two-way radio.

"I have an injured domestic rabbit that needs a vet," the policewoman said into the microphone.

"I don't give a damn about any old rabbit," the voice interrupted. "Take it to Animal Control."

"Sir, I think vet care—"

"I said, ANIMAL CONTROL."

The loud, unfriendly tone scared the rabbit. He tucked in on himself, getting as small as he could, pressing his ears flat against his shoulders.

"Yes, sir," the woman answered quietly, clicking off her microphone.

Then, speaking to her furry passenger, she said, "Animal Control doesn't have much space right now, and I couldn't stand it if you were killed. Don't worry, little bunny. I've got a plan."

The patrol car followed the beam of its headlights through darkened neighborhoods and into the outskirts of the Colorado town. The six-month-old bunny tensed when the vehicle stopped.

His crate was lifted and suddenly the rabbit was in. . .a chicken coop! His ears swiveled and his sensitive nose wiggled as he took in the unfamiliar sounds and smells.

"I'm guessing you aren't going to be too pleased with this arrangement," the woman told him. "But it's the best I can do tonight."

She cleaned and blocked off one corner of the coop, put hay and a bowl of fresh water down on the floor, and then let the rabbit out of the carrier.

"I don't think you'll get sick from just one night with the chickens," she whispered as she petted his nose. "I'll see you in the morning."

Hours later, as the light of dawn began seeping into the chicken house, his new friend returned. "The House Rabbit Society folks are going to take care of you, little one," she said happily.

The car ride didn't seem so fearful this time; he trusted the human who chauffeured him to the Denver metro area. A lady named Bea was waiting for them. The rabbit relaxed as he listened to the friendly voices.

Bea opened the carrier and scooped him up. "Oh! Poor baby!" she exclaimed. "Look at the mangled flesh on his neck and face. And his eye—he can't close it. What happened to him?"

"I don't know, Bea," the officer replied glumly. "I found him cowering at the side of a road."

"I'll get him to my vet right away."

The patrolwoman petted the bunny one last time. He licked her fingers in thanks, then willingly let Bea put him in a carrier.

"Your name will be Frankie," she told him as they started the drive.

Within an hour, Frankie was in the hands of Bea's trusted vet. After thoroughly examining the rabbit, he shook his head, then said solemnly, "Someone put a rope around this rabbit's neck and swung him around. Abscesses have developed in the rope-burn wounds. The injuries have stretched the skin on his face, which is why the eyelid isn't working."

Frankie's extensive injuries required surgery that day. The abscesses were cleaned and the skewed eyelid fixed so that it would shut. By the time Bea picked Frankie up that evening, his nails were trimmed and fur combed. He looked wonderful, in spite of the sores circling his neck and marring his face.

When Bea put Frankie into the room prepared for him, he knew he was safe. He began kissing her face, licking her with love and gratitude. She laughed with delight as the soft, barely damp tongue groomed every part of her that was within reach.

Frankie turned out to be the perfect houseguest—his behavior was so impeccable that he was soon allowed to roam at will. His favorite activity was to follow his new best friend everywhere, even when it required jumping three-foot baby gates!

It was only when Bea remained stationary for a time that Frankie dashed off to explore every nook and cranny he could find. He ignored the soreness of his face and neck and turned every room into a dance parlor, dashing, leaping, and springing into the air to kick sideways or to spin around. He seemed to be saying, "Forget the *bad* people; I'm with *good* people. Everything is wonderful! *REJOICE!*" His positive outlook bounced through the house with him.

But when Bea called his name, he rushed to her, eager to be picked up and cuddled. He was content to sit on her lap for hours at a time, alternately tooth purring and grooming her. In return for his presence, he *demanded* that she pet him. Bea always smiled at him and teased, "You have a weakness for love!"

One cold November day, the five-pound bunny was healed enough to be taken on a very special excursion—to the television studio of the local NBC affiliate.

Frankie was one of several adoptable rabbits Bea wished to showcase. Seconds before the cameras rolled, she handed him to the anchorman conducting the interview. Frankie was happy to receive gentle caresses and sat sedately in place, eliciting comments about his charming personality.

When the segment ended, the newsman made the "mistake" of reaching to shake hands with Bea instead of continuing to pet Frankie. In the flash of an eye, the rabbit nipped his arm, telling the man in no uncertain terms that he expected to be petted *nonstop*. Startled, the poor fellow leapt to his feet, dumping Frankie into Bea's arms.

Bea wasn't sure who was more surprised, she or the anchorman. *Thank goodness we're off camera*, was her first thought.

She conveyed both apology and humor as she quickly explained Frankie's need for affection. She was relieved when the newsman laughingly forgave Frankie and labeled his penchant for petting as "Frankie's foible."

Frankie's public appearance generated viewer interest. As much as Bea loved his company, she was happy when a family chose him and three other rabbits for adoption. She helped introduce the four bunnies to one another, and a few days later the group was ensconced in their own room, in their new forever home.

Now Frankie thinks he's in heaven: he has human *and* bunny friends to give him love and attention. His penchant for petting hasn't changed one bit. When he craves human contact, he runs up and nudges an ankle. After someone caters to his request, Frankie lavishly bestows bunny kisses. It's his way of happily admitting, "I have a weakness for love!"

ABOUT RABBITS: creating a trusted friendship

Some rabbits love to be held and petted; they will sit on their human's lap, tooth-purring in contentment. Other rabbits may prefer to receive petting and affection while seated next to their human on the floor. Still others seem to hate being held or fondled and may scrabble to get away.

Becoming a bunny's trusted friend requires time and effort and the awareness of what it means to be a prey animal. The amount of socialization bunnies receive when young influences their reactions to humans. Rabbits are less stressed when they are familiar with family activities and when their condos are respected as private spaces.

When rabbits run away from someone or prepare to defend themselves, it may be because they do not trust that person. In human-rabbit relationships, humans must not only *be* trustworthy, but must also convince the rabbits that they *are* trustworthy.

Regardless of how much he or she may enjoy your company, do not expect your bunny to love attention as much as Frankie. Few rabbits will come when called and many do not "kiss." It is important to respect each rabbit's uniqueness and to never expect a bunny to act like an affectionate dog.

A Treasure Found

Information for this story was provided by Caroline Gilbert

November in Hilton Head, South Carolina, was a perfect time to be in the coastal resort community: the humidity was lower, most of the tourists were gone, hurricane season was coming to an end. Life on the island was returning to normal.

Except for one small bunny.

Paralyzed with fear, he hunched next to a cardboard box that had fallen from the dumpster.

Someone had taken him to the forsaken place and left him there.

Alone.

With neither food nor water.

His long ears registered danger and he flattened himself against the box, attempting invisibility. He remained motionless, instinctively knowing that, if detected, he might be killed.

His buff-colored fur helped shield him. A person ran past with a dog. Neither noticed the cowering creature.

A man and his six-year-old son, enjoying an early-morning nature walk, sauntered into view. The young bunny stayed frozen in place, but the tall man spotted him.

Amos recognized that the rabbit was not a native wild one, and he knew that a domestic bunny would not survive on his own. After explaining to Chandler how they might capture the small waif, he and the boy began ambling toward the garbage area.

The terrified bunny darted behind the dumpster. Young Chandler spied him and started forward again; Amos circled around to approach from behind.

The rabbit bolted from one side to the other.

Father and son worked together, herding the rabbit, trying to get close. But the bunny was scared and kept scrambling away.

Thirty minutes passed. Then forty. The rabbit was tiring. Talking in quiet tones, Amos slowly walked up to face the bunny, leaned over, and gently petted between the rabbit's dark brown eyes. The little rex was too tired to run away and momentarily relaxed—just long enough for Amos to grasp him firmly.

Amos lifted the wisp of a rabbit and checked him over. The short fur was soiled and dull. The rabbit was too skinny; he was starving and dehydrated.

"He needs medical care."

"Let's take him to Grandma," Chandler said.

"He might belong to somebody," Amos hedged.

"He's all alone," his son countered.

"Maybe he's lost."

"Huh-uh. I don't see anyone looking for him."

The child's logic was irrefutable. There was not a soul in sight. Nor any houses nearby. Amos knew the vulnerable prey animal had not traveled to the area on his own.

They hurried to the car, where Amos settled the little rabbit on his son's lap. He drove through the nearest residential area, but found no one outside frantically searching for a cherished bunny companion.

Amos called his mother, Caroline Gilbert, founder and manager of the Rabbit Sanctuary in Simpsonville, South Carolina. Soon they were on their way, taking the rex rabbit to his new home.

Chandler stroked the amiable bunny's head and back. It was obvious the rabbit enjoyed the tender ministrations—he snuggled closer to his human buddy.

Caroline Gilbert

Caroline Gilbert

"He's the color of toast, Dad. I'm going to call him Toast."

As though in answer, the bunny butted his head against Chandler's hand, wanting more caresses.

"Look, Dad—he loves to be petted." Then the child's voice turned serious. "Toast would've died if we hadn't found him, right?"

"Yes, he would."

Chandler pensively stroked the soft fur, then declared, "It's good we took that walk this morning."

Upon arrival at the sanctuary, Toast's health checkup revealed digestive problems serious enough to make him a permanent resident of the health care building. Chandler helped settle the nine-month-old bunny, chattering to his grandmother about the rescue and how much Toast liked being petted.

The very next day Caroline verified Chandler's assertions; she found out that Toast basked in attention! The new resident was sweet and charming, and he thoroughly enjoyed having people run their fingers through his cotton-velvet fur. It didn't take long for him to earn the distinction of the bunny most often virtually adopted (meaning he never had to leave home). Chandler would visit and quip that Toast was one of his grandmother's best treasures.

But despite Toast's fondness for people, it was Emily who became the love of his life. A diminutive silver-grey rabbit, she was brought to the sanctuary by a gentleman who loved her well but who worked long hours and knew she was lonely. Because of physical problems, she was assigned to the health building. Toast instinctively sensed Emily's frailty and for several years was her steadfast companion, her comfort and protector.

When Emily died, Caroline was so concerned that Toast would become depressed by the loss of his beloved that she and other volunteers spent extra time with him. So effectively did Toast's human friends help him through his loneliness that when Roanoke, a head-tilt bunny, and Toby, an older rabbit with health problems, took up residence, Toast willingly extended his nose in friendship. The three friends began to spend their time together, inside and out.

Toast is an elderly rabbit now. Although he is somewhat creaky and less spry, age has not diminished his fondness for attention. He is one of the first rabbits that sanctuary visitors see, and he makes sure he gets what he considers a fair share of the petting. When Chandler and Amos visit, Toast gingerly hops over to be picked up. They are always willing to comply. After all, they were the first to recognize Toast for the treasure he is.

ABOUT RABBITS: vision

Although rabbits' eyes are structured to see in dim light and to give a panoramic view, they are unable to recognize detail or to perceive a full color spectrum. Rabbits stand on their hind legs to identify surroundings, recognize distant objects, and discern danger.

Because the eyes are located on the sides of their heads, rabbits do not have binocular vision. To compensate, they "bob" (move their heads up and down) or "scan" (turn their heads from side to side). These movements somewhat alter their observational position and provide a new line of sight (parallax).

In addition, their eye placement creates two blind spots—a short one in front of the face and a longer one behind the tail. The blind spot in front of a bunny's nose can lead to inadvertently biting a finger, especially if a bunny smells food or reacts to the "foreign" object as a possible threat.

Due to selective breeding, some domestic rabbits have eyesight that is further limited (in range and acuity) by lop ears, ridged brows, or bangs.

The Rabbit MaMaa Triumphant

Information for this story was provided by Ray Silja, Stephen Guida, and Stacey Shirer

Some young kids found them: the mother rabbit and her eight newborn babies, boxed up and tossed into a dumpster.

The doe was skinny and dirty. Her kits, curled in minuscule balls, were furless, with eyes that looked pasted shut. The kids feared that some of the babies were already dead and, seeking help, hurried the box home.

The bunny family—each member dangerously close to death—was transferred to Brambley Hedge Rabbit Rescue. Founder, Erika, and fellow volunteer, Stacey, worked feverishly to save their lives. It was a relief when MaMaa—as they named her—finally responded with enough strength to tend her tiny babies.

But that respite was short-lived. Less than two weeks after being rescued, every one of the kits became critically ill. Again death threatened.

The vet discovered a massive infestation of parasites. Obviously MaMaa had endured horrible living conditions in her early life and had passed the parasites to her offspring. Medication was necessary, and Erika worried about the sizable risk of long-term effects to the young ones.

An entire week passed before all the babies began to show signs of improvement. A sense of optimism again filled the shelter.

Then—only twenty-nine days after the rabbits had been discovered in the trash—the still-thin MaMaa birthed more babies. The timing made it clear that MaMaa had been newly pregnant when she and her eight nurslings were discarded. The only bright note, if it could be called that, was that the new litter was small, due to MaMaa's poor health.

So that she could care for her newborns, Erika and Stacey weaned the first litter of eight, diligently providing the extra care needed at that young age.

But despite their ministrations, illness again set in and death prevailed for four of the bunnies. Among those survivors strong enough to battle the ravages of their early lives, some exhibited signs of congenital problems, making them special-needs bunnies.

Finally, good fortune conquered adversity. MaMaa recovered, acquiring self-assurance as rapidly as weight. Golden fur—highlighted by white—became a luxurious covering for her eight-pound body. Her remaining youngsters, gorgeous miniatures of their upright-eared palomino-mix mother, grew to health and were adopted. Although independent, MaMaa loved attention and was so sweet and loving that Erika and Stacey were sure that she too would soon find herself in a forever home.

But four years passed. MaMaa was continually overlooked in favor of smaller bunnies or lop-eared breeds.

Then, at long last, a special day. Brambley Hedge received an email from a man who had lost his beloved French lop, Janis. With tears blurring her vision, Stacey read, "Although I have a special affection for lops, I prefer to adopt any breed so long as the rabbit is one nobody else wants and is, therefore, unlikely to be selected."

She immediately wrote back, describing MaMaa and two other rabbits, and arranged to meet Ray at PetSmart on a scheduled adoption day.

~

Ray remembers his first sight of MaMaa: "She was lying down, resting her head on the edge of her litter box. She looked so cute and relaxed. When I walked up, she hopped to the cage door, curious about me."

He completed the necessary adoption requirements, and MaMaa finally went home.

But instead of feeling safe in her new surroundings, MaMaa acted frightened of everything. The sound of Ray clearing his throat sent her running to hide under the bed. The sight of a grooming brush brought a wild look to her eyes, and she'd attack, as though fearing Ray intended to hit her with it. If he made a sudden movement, she lunged and drew blood.

With sadness he wrote, "I suspect she suffered abuse at the hands of a male. It's going to take a long time before those bad memories subside."

But Ray persevered, even spending months sleeping on the floor with MaMaa to help her get used to him. It took over a year before she fully relaxed into comfort and security. Once she did, she blossomed!

She would rise early with Ray and, before the desert heated up, dart in and out of the house, making a game of racing to the best hiding spots in the rabbit-fenced yard. Her guardian watched as she performed gymnastics, dug holes, and then snoozed under the sunscreen drape.

When it became too hot, she would come inside, lying next to Ray so he could pet her while he read. When it was time for him to leave for class—retired now and working on a second advanced degree—she'd settle under a chair and listen to classical music on the radio, expressing contentment by softly grinding her teeth, a rabbit's method of purring.

Ray Silja

And she learned words and phrases. Many of them. Ray, whose eclectic background includes co-authorship of a book on literacy tutoring as well as research into animal intelligence, used frequent repetition to nurture and expand her vocabulary. He provided periodic updates to Stacey, extolling the intelligence of The Rabbit MaMaa, who also recognized her names, "Baby" and "Sweetheart."

Given affection and freedom, MaMaa has become a carefree, well-adjusted rabbit. When she's happy and excited, she spins in circles at Ray's feet. When she observes that he plans to lie on the floor and watch television, she gets in position for petting. MaMaa has turned into a cuddler who can't spend enough time with the man who respects her and holds her dear.

The two now share their home with a couple of Netherland dwarfs. Though MaMaa adores the small bunnies, she eschews their flurry of activity, choosing instead to sit with her trusted human.

Her days are filled with ease and joy—the adversity endured as a young doe long forgotten. Hers is a success story, and she is The Rabbit MaMaa Triumphant.

ABOUT RABBITS: reproduction

Rabbits can begin reproducing at a surprisingly young age. Some rabbits may achieve sexual maturity as early as 2-1/2 months, even though 4 months is considered standard. Rabbits should never be bred at a young age, as this practice creates problems in both mother and offspring.

Female rabbits do not have specific fertility cycles—no timing is involved. The act of mating causes them to ovulate (induced ovulation) and pregnancy is nearly guaranteed. The gestation period for rabbits is basically a month (28–31 days).

A healthy doe can deliver 1–14 babies; the average number born to a mid-size rabbit is 6 or 7. The first litter is generally smaller. A rabbit can become pregnant shortly after giving birth, but that is incredibly stressful and unhealthy for the doe and her kits.

When "same sex" rabbits are purchased, there is often a rude surprise when baby bunnies are subsequently born. This often happens because it is difficult to properly sex young rabbits. The fact that testicles of young males are commonly carried inside their bodies leads inexperienced observers to assume that they are females. Even if the male is immediately removed after discovery of his gender, a litter is often born about 30 days later.

Of course, all these situations can be avoided if much-loved bunnies are accurately sexed and kept gender-separated from the age of 10 weeks until spayed or neutered, at the appropriate age and by a rabbit-knowledgeable vet.

Born to Be *ME!*

by Bernie S. Siegel, MD

It was early spring, just a week after Easter. Two baby rabbits, purchased to adorn Easter baskets, had lost their appeal. They were still cute and cuddly, but taking care of them had become just another chore.

The children's parents didn't want the responsibility of caring for the bunnies. So, under the cover of twilight the two tiny babies, who could easily fit into a coat pocket, were abandoned in the nearby woods.

In near darkness, the defenseless orphans crouched together, quivering with fear. The rustling sounds, menacing dark shadows, strange and disturbing smells—everything about the alien place heightened their panic and instincts to hide.

But the two little sisters had no burrow to hide in. No food or water. They had no family to turn to, no one to help them. The dark fur of one bunny helped hide her in the darkness. The other tiny rabbit was white and her fur, illuminated by the moon, was like a beacon for predators. She did not survive the night.

The small black bunny, nearly scared to death, was left to face the nightmare of the woods alone. She hunched under a bush, paralyzed with fear and grieving for her sister and only friend; she was depressed, hungry, thirsty, cold.

Dawn came at last. The baby rabbit caught the scent of food. Heedless of danger, she followed the smell. It emanated from a nearby wire contraption where, upon entering, she found a bowl of baby bunny pellets. Just as her mouth touched the dish the trap snapped closed behind her.

The rabbit whirled around. There was no way out.

~

"She looks like a little black smudge," my wife, Bobbie, observed.

And so, in that moment, our rabbit was named: *Smudge.*

Bobbie and I had happened to see the abrupt abandonment of the two bunnies the night before and had immediately tried to save them. But since they were afraid and retreated further into the darkness, we set a humane trap.

Early the next morning, we hurried to check it. The coal-black bunny was inside, hunched down, trying to hide.

"We're buddies," I said as I opened the cage.

Her elfin body, so downy soft, fit into the palm of my hand. I'd never held a rabbit in this way before and was immediately awestruck. She was so perfect. I felt my heart open in wonder and gratitude.

Gazing at the vulnerable little creature, I marveled at how she sat so trustingly in my hand. She looked at me with her beautiful brown eyes, and I knew she was a blessing, and more—her presence was an opportunity to learn.

I was sure our four cats would come to accept Smudge, but I wondered how those feline predators would initially react to the sudden appearance of a helpless prey animal. Keeping our newest family member safe became my first objective. I built a sturdy, predator-proof, three-room bunny bungalow and secured it on an outside porch, in front of our windows so we could see Smudge at all times.

She appeared content and seemed to enjoy the attention from the curious cats, who liked to sit next to her home. After everyone became good friends, they shared the yard whenever Bobbie or I was able to watch and keep them safe.

As Smudge grew, it became apparent she would eclipse the size of the cats and become a very large rabbit. In addition, she was so congenial and exhibited such a loving and intelligent nature that Bobbie and I wanted her to be inside with us. And so she became a house rabbit.

What a surprise that turned out to be—living so closely with Smudge really opened our eyes about rabbits! We had read books and searched the Internet about rabbit care, but it was through Smudge that we gained a new level of understanding and appreciation for them. It was a startling revelation to find out that our sweet and gentle prey animal was also very independent, mischievous, and bold. Sometimes Smudge tried my patience, leading me on a merry chase before bedtime instead of coming into the house. Bobbie would tease, saying our rabbit was a lot like me!

One summer day we were introduced to rabbit communication. We heard a grunt—not a soft little sound but a full-throated, hoarse, growly sound, one that had Smudge's full fifteen pounds behind it.

Bobbie started and whirled around; I dropped the morning paper.

Seeing she'd achieved the desired affect, Smudge looked at us and grunted again.

"She must be hungry," Bobbie said as she hurried to wash Smudge's favorite vegetables.

"Maybe she wants to be petted," I responded and got down on the floor to caress her soft fur.

And that is how Bobbie and I were inducted into Smudge's training program.

We learned that our rabbit wanted to be fed at the *same* time every day! When her meal was even a few minutes delayed, Smudge would grunt her annoyance, fling her empty bowl through the air, and watch it clatter noisily across the tiled kitchen floor.

She also liked being held and cuddled *upon request.* I remember the first time Smudge obtained affection on demand. Bobbie and I were in the den, and I guess Smudge thought we were ignoring her. She raced into the room, vaulted onto my lap, grabbed my book and threw it to the floor! When I began to gently stroke her ears and back, she flopped on her side in a big body smile and totally relaxed.

Smudge was always forthright in asking for attention and love—and she always expected to receive it. I'd urge my cancer patients, many of whom have a hard time asking for love, to emulate Smudge's assertiveness.

Smudge's instruction didn't stop when we learned what she liked; she imparted other important life lessons. One of her greatest teachings occurred when I unintentionally let her come to harm. It happened after I came home from the shelter with a little abandoned dog, whom Bobbie promptly dubbed Furphy. Knowing that Smudge was a vulnerable prey animal, we were careful to supervise their interactions. Furphy was a playful and sweet dog, and we made progress with the training.

One afternoon Bobbie and I had to do a few errands, and after we left the house I remembered I hadn't closed the pet door. But I thought Furphy and Smudge were good enough friends, so I wasn't really worried.

When we returned home, Smudge was in her house, injured. Furphy had attacked her, and I couldn't understand why because they had played together before. Had he, in his exuberant dog way, tried playing with her as if she were a stuffed toy?

Smudge's wounds were serious and required surgery. The guilt I felt about this was enormous. My life has been spent trying to cure disease and help people heal, but because of my error in judgment, our loving, innocent rabbit had been harmed. I was the one who had wanted a dog and brought Furphy home. I loved them both, but I felt I'd seriously failed in my duty and responsibility to Smudge.

After she was home from the animal hospital, as the doctor in the house I provided all her care myself. Each morning and evening, I gave her medication and fluids, swabbed and dressed her wounds, made sure she was clean and dry, and hand-fed a special dietary formula. Even though I tried to be gentle, I could see it was painful when I tended her injuries or when she attempted to shift positions.

But Smudge never complained. Instead, she was grateful for my care and attention and would lick my hand when I was done.

Each day, I prayed for Smudge and visualized her whole and healthy. My guilt made the process a difficult one. Because of me, Smudge hovered between life and death, and I found it hard to feel joyful.

One evening, after I finished dressing her wounds, I felt the caress of Smudge's smooth tongue. I recognized her unconditional love for me and was finally able to joyfully and spontaneously smile again. I painted a portrait of Smudge and her truth was evident: she was whole and perfect, despite her wounds, and she was helping me to become a more complete human being.

Smudge became my coach and teacher, a perfect example of love and unity with life. At the time, it struck me that the word "wound" kept coming up in various contexts, separate from my life's work of healing wounds. This time, I had to work on that part of me that needed attention. Smudge helped close my wound, the one caused by guilt, and reminded me that blessings come in many forms.

Within a few weeks, Smudge was running and hopping again, with me in attendance. At first, she was afraid of Furphy, but one afternoon when I had to leave and wanted to make sure she was safely indoors, she amazed me by running over to hide behind him. In that simple gesture Smudge demonstrated that she'd forgiven Furphy.

I was so happy she had recovered that I didn't mind being led on a merry chase around the yard. Instead of becoming impatient, I welcomed the opportunity to see her exhibiting such liveliness.

One night, the moon was full and Smudge wanted to stay outside and play. I disagreed because I couldn't see well enough in the moonlight and her dark coat was nearly invisible in the shadows. But when she ran away from me, I followed. She stopped long enough for me to catch up, then leapt and sprinted away. I trailed after her. Again Smudge waited, but when I bent to pick her up, her speedy dash left me empty-handed!

It turned into a game of "chase me in the moonlight." Smudge showed no fear of the night, not even of the large shadows cast by the forest or the haunting and unfamiliar sounds that echoed nearby. She knew she was safe with me.

As the nighttime magic wove around Smudge, I watched my beloved teacher and friend transform into an enchanting dancer: she hopped, spun, and capered with her silhouette. Her choreography signaled her sentiments: "I'm wild. I'm free. I was born to be *ME*!"

And that was another of Smudge's lessons: that I, too, was born to be me, with all my strengths and failings, my loves and fears.

As Smudge danced her finale, I called softly to her. She stopped, rose up on her hind legs, and looked at me. In silent communication we stood.

Then Smudge ran and hopped into my waiting arms. Grateful for her presence in my life, I gathered her close and bent my forehead to hers. The realization that we were both divine children filled me with peace.

Together we entered our home.

ABOUT RABBITS: rabbits as Easter gifts

Baby bunnies are often purchased as cuddly novelties to decorate Easter baskets. But as the small animals begin to grow, they often lose their status as ideal pets. There are some common reasons for this.

- Rabbits are frequently purchased on impulse and without adequate knowledge of their temperament and needs.
- Family members often lose interest after the novelty wears off and when chores become tiresome.
- As rabbits enter adolescence (at about 3-1/2 months old), they become more independent and grow more strongly into instinctive behaviors such as chewing and digging. As they mature, they may become aggressive or grouchy, especially if not neutered or spayed. At this point, family members may begin to view their impulse purchase as a troublesome nuisance, which can lead to abuse, neglect, or abandonment.

Help put a stop to the thoughtless tradition of purchasing live rabbits at Easter. No matter how tempting, never give a bunny as a holiday gift. Encourage family members and friends to reconsider if they are thinking of acquiring a rabbit at Easter. Urge them instead to join you in exuberantly declaring, "Make mine a *chocolate* bunny!"

Note: The Columbus (Ohio) House Rabbit Society established the Make Mine Chocolate!™ *campaign to help educate the public about the problems inherent in purchasing rabbits at Easter. See their website at www.makeminechocolate.org.*

Bunzo

Information for this story was provided by Debby Widolf

Bunzo was obviously ill. His tiny body was rigid, his eyes glassy. Each breath seemed a monumental effort. I reached into the cage at the emergency veterinary clinic and lightly stroked the sweet face of my four-ounce bunny. I was trying to comfort him—and myself.

The veterinarian returned from looking at Bunzo's chest x-rays.

"I'm sorry, but your little rabbit has pneumonia. His physical condition suggests he's been sick for several weeks."

The words shivered fear all the way to my toes; my stomach clutched. Bunzo was only five weeks old. I was afraid he wouldn't survive the illness.

"Please try, little one," I pleaded.

It was a Saturday night. I felt lucky to find an emergency veterinarian knowledgeable about treating rabbits. I tagged along with him as Bunzo was transferred into the animal intensive care unit. The veterinarian explained that the temperature would be controlled to keep Bunzo warm and oxygen would be pumped in to help him breathe. Antibiotics would be administered two ways: nebulized into the air of the chamber and injected into his body.

At least he'd have a fighting chance at survival. But the veterinarian cautioned that pneumonia is often fatal for a rabbit, especially one as young and frail as Bunzo. I knew the medications could also have a deleterious effect on his immature body.

"Keep fighting," I whispered.

I had to leave Bunzo at the emergency clinic that night. In the morning, he'd be transferred to an animal hospital for three days of care. I was leaving with empty arms; my heart felt as though it were breaking.

The next afternoon Bunzo showed very little improvement, and I felt discouraged. After spending time with him, I walked aimlessly, remembering my first sight of the little guy. It was hard to believe that it had been just the week before that I strolled toward a department store at the mall. I had taken one impulsive peek as I passed a pet shop. . .and there he was, cowering in a glass aquarium, trying to hide from the snake coiled in the cage next to his. As I walked up, the large, beautiful bird perched on the bunny's other side voiced a raucous greeting. The bunny quailed at the strident sound.

I focused on the dainty black rabbit with a white diamond on his nose. He was a soft ball of fluff and so cute, just about the sweetest thing I'd ever set eyes on. And so tiny!

My heart was his at first sight. I heard myself saying, "Will you put a hold on him for ten minutes while I go next door? Don't sell him to anyone else."

After we arrived home and Bunzo was settled in, I began researching rabbit care. I was relieved to find answers to many questions the pet-store clerk had been unsure about. Three basics were at the top of my agenda: proper diet, litter training, and Bunzo's safety as he explored new surroundings.

Meanwhile, my impetuous purchase turned into a real bundle of joy! Bunzo bounced around the house, nosing his way into anything and everything he could reach (after I rabbit-proofed, that is). Each day, though, he seemed less lively.

And then he went deathly still.

Now, only a week after I brought him home, I found myself praying Bunzo would survive and brighten my life once again.

On day four, I was delighted when my bunny's status changed from hospital patient to at-home convalescent. But he didn't hop or move around; he just sat stock-still, accepting my nursing care and politely taking his medication in a very unrabbit-like manner.

In a panic, I sought answers. A phone call to the veterinarian brought a prediction of improvement in another week. Sure enough, six days later my adorable bunny took his first tentative steps.

But it was three months before Bunzo was fully recovered. My spontaneous pet store visit had become a frightening and expensive lesson: Bunzo turned out to be a seven-hundred-dollar purchase!

While I nursed Bunzo back to health, I continued to research bunny care and learned the sad truth about his early life. Like many pet-store bunnies, he was weaned from his mother too soon and then his needs were overlooked by the pet store staff. The glass aquarium in which he had been displayed provided inadequate ventilation and had robbed Bunzo's tiny lungs of clean air. I shook my head, remembering that he was housed next to a predator and a clamorous bird. I could imagine how those emotional stresses could also undermine his immune system. The cumulative result of his upbringing was a small body too weak to resist illness.

I vowed that Bunzo would have every opportunity to live a long, happy life, no matter the cost. I repeated my pledge often.

My little one regained strength and started growing; his curiosity, however, outpaced his size. I'd be fawning over him and all of a sudden he'd dart across the room to check out some new object. Or the dryer would chime, and he'd dash to the laundry room, jumping into the clothes basket to play. He loved the sound of the toaster, insisted on helping me make beds, explored every inch of the house, and delighted in finding secret places to take naps.

Bunzo was less than pleased, however, when I visited a rabbit rescue shelter and adopted the "perfect" bunny companion for him. Jasmine, a baby English spot, had been abandoned along with her nine brothers and sisters in Sandia National Forest, east of Albuquerque, New Mexico. Before a Forest Service worker happened upon them, six of the infants had been killed. Jasmine and three littermates were still alive, but wounded and scared.

In her new home, she turned her fears on Bunzo, biting his ear in introduction! My plan was for them to become friends and play together while I was at work. Instead, they hated one another.

But I was more determined than they were; I would *overcome* their enmity. For over two months, my days followed a pattern. Every morning the rabbits had supervised time together. It never failed: I had to separate them almost immediately. Each evening, I took them for a car ride, which created just enough anxiety for them to proclaim a short truce.

One day a rackety truck passed us, causing the two bunnies to seek comfort from each other. Then, Jasmine licked Bunzo's ear, the same one she'd bitten just months before.

"Omigosh, this is going to work!"

Debby Widolf

My loud exclamation startled the rabbits, who looked at me as though I was in the same league as the noisy truck.

When we returned home, I highlighted the date in red on the calendar. According to my calculation, it had taken sixty-five days for Bunzo and Jasmine to forge a friendship. They became inseparable and would lie cheek-to-cheek in beautiful contrast. He was coated in black, with a white nose. She was clothed in white, with some black spots, black ears, and a black nose. Bunzo would race to greet me, giving me a lick to tell me he was happy; Jasmine would race after him, giving him a lick to tell him she loved him. He was gentle and playful and never bit or scratched; she was gentle too, until I had to give Bunzo some medication—then she'd nip me, telling me to be careful with her best friend.

The two of them enlivened the house with their big personalities. They were inquisitive, sweet, sometimes mischievous rabbits who never missed an opportunity to play. Almost anything could be an invitation to leap into action. Their jubilant dance recitals were part ballet, part stunt, and part razzle-dazzle.

Every time I looked at Bunzo and Jasmine, I smiled. What an introduction they provided to the wonderful world of rabbits!

Over the years, many rabbits have enhanced my life, all adopted from shelters or rabbit rescue groups. All are a part of Bunzo's impressive legacy.

And for that I thank him, my black beauty boy.

ABOUT RABBITS: before bringing a bunny home

Small rabbits look like a bundle of love, with their innocent expressions, plush fur, and quiet mannerisms. To many people, the petite animals look like darling little toys. This response leads to bunnies being marketed as cute, cuddly, soft, and sweet.

Seldom are new rabbit parents aware of the real personalities and essential requirements of bunnies. They are high-maintenance animals, with needs that are very different from those of cats and dogs.

Before bringing home a newly adopted or purchased rabbit, research diet, health, behavior, socialization, housing, bunny-proofing, proximity to appropriate vet care—everything! Gather information from rabbit rescue groups and rabbit-knowledgeable veterinarians; also access reputable sites on the Internet and books on house rabbits.

Remember that many bunnies, including purebreds, end up in animal shelters after their cute baby stage ends. If not adopted or transferred to a rescue group, many shelters euthanize them due to space constraints and other issues. If you decide to make a lifetime commitment to a rabbit companion, consider shelters, animal rescue organizations, or pet stores associated with a good rescue group.

The Valiant Voyager

Information for this story was provided by Beverly Endsley, Dr. Jerry LaBonde, Bea LeNoir, and Michael Stein

"This rabbit will never make it."

My heart lurched; my stomach turned.

"I doubt he'll survive surgery on the abscess. . ."

My chest felt like it was being compressed in a vise.

". . .and if he does, Bea, I suspect he won't live more than a week after the surgery."

Tears flooded my eyes, obscuring the image of the pitiful body.

In silence, Jerry, my friend and trusted veterinarian, finished examining the pathetic ragamuffin, barely recognizable as a rabbit.

But the poor bunny looks better than he did a few hours ago, I reminded myself.

Hours earlier, I had received a late-night call from a woman frantic to locate help for a rabbit who had dragged himself into her backyard. After receiving directions to our shelter, the wonderful humanitarian had driven over an hour to deliver the bunny.

"He's in terrible condition," she said as she handed me the make-do carrier: a box punched with breathing holes. Pale and distraught, she watched as I opened it.

My throat constricted as I looked at the dirty, skinny, stinky lump of fur. Ears identified him as a rabbit, but his lower teeth grew out from his face like tusks. Four-inches long, covered with dirt and feces, they stuck straight out. The top incisors, the same length, grew out to the sides like a strange mustache. A pus-filled, baseball-sized lump masked his jaw, adding to the grotesque look of his head.

Severely starved and dehydrated, the rest of the rabbit's body was a grouping of sharp-edged bones, every angle visible. Feces matted his fur; urine burn blistered his legs; bloody sores riddled his feet. Toenails were either broken or twisted in unnatural directions. Mite-infested fur fell off in clumps, leaving bare skin where his beautiful coat should have been. A black, tarry mess discharged from his ears, evidence of ear mites.

"Is he still alive?" The rescuer's question echoed her distress.

"Just barely." I could hardly get the words out.

Lifting the rabbit from the box would have caused him intense pain, so I cut away a side of the carton. The rabbit cringed, afraid of my hands—or of my mere presence.

He needed emergency care and, despite his distrust, I had to work on his pitiful body: administering pain medication, clipping nails, hydrating subcutaneously, cutting back the teeth, syringing food, medicating the rabbit's legs and feet, applying bandages, and treating him for mites.

I took him home, hoping we would both get some restorative sleep. But my thoughts badgered me so that I couldn't rest. *He might not live more than a few hours. He should not have to die alone. His last moments should be filled with gentleness and love.* And the ubiquitous, but pointless, questions that plague rescuers in any cruelty situation: *How could anyone allow such a thing? Why would anyone let a defenseless being suffer like that?*

Although the rabbit gave evidence of wanting to live, each labored breath seemed it would be his last. I was afraid to close my eyes lest he die while I catnapped.

"You're so brave and beautiful," I told him over and over as I gently held him, wanting him to know kindness, even if only for a short time.

He lived through the night.

"Bea?" Jerry's voice jerked me back to the examining room of the veterinary hospital. He was waiting for my decision, his compassion tangible.

He's NOT going to die.

The words impacted me from out of nowhere. I drew on their strength.

"He's not going to die, Jerry," I said with conviction.

He nodded in sympathetic understanding and quietly went to work. After administering additional fluids, Jerry clipped the fur, cleaned the skin sores, and surgically lanced and drained the abscess as completely as possible.

"We've already discussed pain medication. Give him a bicillin injection every other day and bring him back in a week. I'll do surgery then," he said when he finished the procedures.

I was thankful Jerry didn't add the obvious: "If he's still alive."

Once home, I laid the rabbit's withered body in the bassinet that once held my child, healthy and so filled with life. Now in her place lay a being so weak he could not lift his head.

He's not going to die. I welcomed the reassuring words.

After administering his medications, there was nothing more I could do but give him a name—Buddy—and breathe a prayer for his safety and healing.

"Buddy," I sang out with false confidence the next morning as I peeked around the corner.

His eyes were focused in my direction.

I gave him time to become accustomed to my presence, then gathered him close, grateful he'd lived through another night. He rested limply in my arms, too feeble to struggle in fear. There was a quietness about him too, as though he realized fate had brought him where he would be cared for.

Very gently, trying not to cause him unnecessary pain, I began the intensive home-care regimen: fluids under the skin twice a day, syringe-feeding every few hours, medications, and changing the bandages on his legs and feet.

Buddy accepted it all in stoic silence as he teetered at the edge of death. Even there, he remembered fear. But he remembered life too: he would try to groom his front paws and eat his food, signs of his strong will to live.

Beverly Endsley

"You're safe now and so brave," I would tell him, extolling his obvious courage. Somehow he had escaped from a living hell.

I recited nursery rhymes, just as I did when my daughter was a baby: "If wishes were horses. . . ." I'd see a barely perceptible twitch and would cling to the hope that he was responding.

A week later Jerry performed the surgery, which exposed a menacing reality: the abscess had eaten into a large portion of Buddy's jaw. The infected bone had to be removed, leaving a gaping wound. After that, Jerry extracted the four rotted and malformed front teeth.

Buddy lived through the surgery.

When I arrived to take him home, Jerry cautioned, "The abscess was one of the worst I've ever seen; it's likely to recur and destroy Buddy's entire jaw." His voice softened, "Bea, you know how slim the chances are for a rabbit to survive this kind of damage. Given Buddy's weak and compromised state, he probably won't live much longer."

But despite the poor prognosis, the bicillin injections were continued. Because Buddy was in such grave condition and the chance of his recovery was so bleak, the standard rabbit protocol of one dose every other day was changed to a daily injection.

I did what I could to comfort Buddy and give him strength. If he lived, I knew it would be a miracle, and not of my making.

I watched his valiant struggle to live compete with the threat of death.

I gauged time in small, but significant, ways. Three days after the surgery, Buddy tried to lift his head to receive food from the syringe. He was not very successful, but he tried.

"Good for you!"

Another four days passed: Buddy lifted his head and then tried to sit up! He tipped over before I could assist him, landing softly in the bassinet, but it was a start.

WOW!

One memorable day in August, just two weeks and two days after being rescued, Buddy greeted me with bright eyes. I saw nary the slightest flinch of fear when I went to pick him up.

My softly murmured, "You little darling," merged into my sigh of relief and joy.

Three weeks passed. Buddy steadfastly clung to life, but he was still in very critical condition. As much as I hated to give him up, it was time for him to go live with Beverly and Kerry. They provided hospice care, and I knew they would make sure Buddy lived the remainder of his days in pampered peace.

"We don't know how much longer Buddy will live."

Bea's words reverberated through my head with aching force.

"We are trying an emergency protocol, but don't get your hopes up."

It felt as though my heart were being wrenched apart.

"He may have a good day but then succumb the next. His abscess was very extensive and is likely to return. If you can just keep him comfortable, Beverly, until—"

Tears clouded my vision. But I could still see Buddy in my mind's eye: the feeble, bony rabbit who needed a loving, safe place to die.

"Kerry and I will do all we can," was all I could choke out.

With a heavy heart I listened to my friend Bea's instructions: pain medication, bicillin injections daily, subcutaneous hydration morning and evening, hand-feeding regularly during the day, cleaning and re-bandaging sore feet, grooming his ill-smelling body, and checking for signs of the abscess.

After Bea lovingly bade Buddy goodbye, I took him home and helped my husband, Kerry, set up a padded cage. As providers of hospice and foster care for the Colorado House Rabbit Society, we had done this many times. But never for a rabbit in such dire condition.

Buddy's pink eyes followed our movements, vigilant for any threatening gestures. Pale-gray nose and ears heeded any changes in our intentions.

Slowly I approached his travel carrier. I was a stranger, and Buddy had good reason to be distrustful of humans.

He cowered, as though expecting blows.

Such evidence of abuse was nearly my undoing. My tears threatened to spill over.

No one should die without having experienced the joys of life.

The words came out of nowhere. I felt them to my core. Buddy deserved every chance to know happiness.

Offering promises of safety, I gently retrieved the little urchin from the carrier and set him on a clean towel on the couch. He tried to make himself vanish from his new, unfamiliar surroundings and, when he could not, began a horrible quaking.

Kerry and I got down on bended knees, making ourselves appear smaller. With feather-light touches, we massaged Buddy's ailing body until it gave up some of its tension. Before bed, we pushed the injection needle though his damaged skin, then offered a silent prayer for his survival.

The next morning, I could not bring myself to open the door to his room. *Is he still alive?*

Kerry turned the knob. Not until he turned to me with a smile did I realize I was holding my breath.

That became the morning routine. Wondering if Buddy made it through the night. Waiting for Kerry's smile.

In the evenings, we took turns administering the bicillin injections, grateful when the emergency daily-dose was replaced by the standard every-other-day dose.

Our days took on a pattern of sorts. Bea had told us about the nursery rhymes she'd recited; we opted to fill our house with music and sometimes I would make up little ditties around the words, "If wishes were horses."

Buddy seemed to respond, or so we desperately wanted to believe.

My passion for oil painting took a back seat to caring for him and our other rabbits, but when I had time, I would paint figures of shadow and light—horses for Buddy. Kerry worked at home when he could, sitting with the rabbits while reviewing architectural drawings. Weekends turned into "bunny spa" days, held in our backyard. Buddy lay in the grass while we, his attendants, groomed him with soft cloths.

We celebrated each small step toward happiness.

He began to relax and enjoy our attention!

We rejoiced.

Buddy took his first unaided step!

We were his cheering squad.

Beautiful white fur began growing in, and markings, once light-gray, turned to near-black. Buddy began to look like the big, handsome Californian-breed rabbit he was meant to be. We were proud parents, snapping photos and showing them to family and friends.

One bright summer day we were sitting under the quaking aspens, watching the chipmunks run back and forth to their home in the rocks. Buddy started grooming his cute black nose with his forepaws. He remained upright and balanced the entire time!

"Way to go!" Kerry exclaimed.

And yet another unforgettable day: Buddy hopped around the backyard and ran through the large cardboard play-tube. Then repeated the accomplishment.

"Yea, Buddy!" We applauded his high-spirited antics.

One day in September, a few months after his heroic journey into the backyard of his rescuer, Buddy performed his first bunny binky. A leap into the air, with a twist. It was a fitting gift for my husband, who celebrated his birthday that same day.

But the specter of death, in the form of the abscess, was never far away; it was step-in-step with Buddy's improvements. We knew each day could be his last. But, oh, how we hoped otherwise. Our sweet little hospice fellow was gaining weight and his jaw was better. However, Jerry, the veterinarian, reminded us that Buddy was still in critical condition.

Bea, who received regular updates about Buddy, suggested a perfect bunny companion: Savannah, a gray lop who had been discarded by her people. Bea assisted with bonding the two rabbits and, as soon as they were good friends, returned them to our house. Sweet-tempered Savannah immediately began her healing ministrations; she nurtured and groomed Buddy, seldom leaving his side.

In early November, we took the bunny couple to be examined by Jerry. He was amazed to see the difference in Buddy and teasingly asked: "You didn't switch rabbits on me, did you?" He answered his own question. "No, here's the scarred area where the abscess was."

Then Jerry gave us the most wonderful news: the abscess had cleared. Death was in abeyance.

Our relief was immense.

But Jerry cautioned us that the abscess could, and probably would, return.

NO! My mind closed against that possibility.

On a late November weekend, Denver's NBC-affiliated television station featured Buddy and Savannah on the

Beverly Endsley

morning news. Buddy captivated the news team and crew, especially after they heard about his valiant struggle.

Following the TV appearance and during the time we were screening potential adopters, Bea paired Buddy and Savannah with another bunny couple: Monique, a deaf head-tilt bunny who had survived against horrible odds, and her partner, Colin. It was a success—now there were four bonded rabbits to comfort and care for one another.

And then a perfect New Year's Day: I received a telephone call from a man whose Californian rabbit had died and who wanted to adopt special-needs bunnies. I described Buddy and his friends. The caller, Mike, said, "I'd like to adopt the four." There was more good news: Mike is a paramedic and also a pilot whose job it is to fly almost daily to Denver—the bunnies would be in able hands and also continue to receive veterinary care from Jerry.

I remember hanging up the phone, thinking, "These rabbits have certainly earned their wings!"

After all the adoption requirements were fulfilled, arrangements were made with a hotel near Denver International Airport. We arrived at the appointed time on January 19 and were shown to the room of Captain Mike.

"Buddy seems to be doing fine now, Mike, but the abscess could return."

I was stunned as I listened to Beverly and Kerry chronicle Buddy's life.

"Savannah and Colin are quite healthy. Monique and Buddy will always require additional care."

My heart swelled as I looked at the four rabbits who would be sharing my Wyoming home. They were so beautiful, albeit frightened by the unfamiliar surroundings, including me.

"They're all very loving, especially Buddy. He's so gentle and grateful, all heart and spirit. How he ever escaped his hellish prison, we'll never know."

I focused on Buddy, looking at me. It was hard to believe that, when he was sick and weighing only a few pounds, he had dragged himself to safety. What a story!

It was after midnight before I gathered all the pertinent information about the four rabbits. At 4:00 a.m., it was time for us to leave. Hotel personnel were helpful and gracious; they peeked at the rabbits in the carrier and added their good wishes for a safe trip.

On the way to the airport, I told my four furry passengers about the aircraft that would soar into the heavens and take us safely home. As scared as they all were, I thought I saw Buddy's upright ears rotate ever so slightly. I took it as a sign that he was listening.

My long-eared travelers were strapped into their assigned place: the jump seat of the cockpit. Monique had had a seizure just hours before, so as a precaution I set an oxygen mask on "full" and placed it inside the carrier. Five miles over the surface of the earth, I checked on them: three were on "full alert." The fourth, deaf little Monique, seemed content, unaffected by the flight or the oxygen mask.

Maggie, my beagle-mix companion of some years, welcomed us home and impatiently waited for me to open the carrier. Her job, as she sees it, is to protect all rabbits, and she immediately conveyed her benevolent intentions.

She watched as I set up a special padded area for frail Monique, who was unable to hop. Then Maggie turned her friendly attention to the other three rabbits. I was amazed that within the hour, Buddy, Savannah, and Colin were following old Maggie around and exploring—no lack of courage in this bunch! With Buddy in the lead and me in tow, they headed out the kitchen door and into the bunny-proofed backyard.

This was January in Wyoming, mind you, and *COLD*! After a half hour, I called it quits and started my training program. "Home," I said and pointed to the door.

They pointedly ignored me.

"Home," I repeated.

In unison, three bunnies presented their backsides to me.

I think it was sweet-dog Maggie who convinced them to take pity on me. A few minutes later they were kind enough to dash inside so I could get warm.

The questionable effectiveness of my training program niggled at me—I wondered who was going to train whom. But, as days passed, it got easier. Buddy thought Maggie-dog was tops, so he followed her around. Colin, who suffers a case of hero worship, fell in behind Buddy, and Savannah brought up the rear. I carried Monique.

Socializing the group was an even simpler task: I enlisted the hearts, hands, and laps of my friends. Each lap was (and still is) assigned a rabbit. Even my card-playing buddies became involved—massages and petting were dealt out *before* attention turned to the game. However, when my friends were not visiting, I had my hands full. The rabbits all needed regular, individual attention.

After I developed a routine, the rabbits established theirs. Buddy loved exploring; he'd lead and his friends would follow. He would investigate everything and staked his claim by chin rubbing—leaving an undetectable-to-humans scent on those things, including Maggie, that Buddy considered part of his territory.

Then, without any warning, the abscess returned and Buddy took a serious downturn. For months, the abscess seesawed in and out of his life. Each time, I flew him to Denver, where House Rabbit Society volunteers assisted me in getting him to and from Jerry's office. Buddy accepted the medical treatment with grace, and his indomitable will to live brought him through. I found it amazing that he would gallop to me when I called his name, even though it meant getting a shot. He was so happy to have his ears scratched and receive attention that he viewed the push of the needle as just another opportunity to spend time on my lap.

He became my inspiration and hero. Everyone who met him felt the same way.

Then, the abscess attacked again, this time with a vengeance. Buddy's body did not respond to the antibiotics.

That evening he was my jump-seat passenger on the trip to Denver. His former hospice parents, Beverly and Kerry, were waiting for us at the airport; they took Buddy to see Jerry at the animal hospital the next morning.

Jerry called me with the devastating news: the abscess once more involved the jawbone, and this time a back tooth was infected as well. He'd already performed the surgery, but my courageous bunny friend was in very grave condition.

Death was again a haunting prospect.

My spirits ebbed. Buddy was such a special rabbit; he meant the world to me. I wasn't prepared to lose him.

He's going to LIVE! The proclamation swept around me like the Wyoming wind.

I took the words to heart and couldn't wait to get Buddy home to start the daily injections. But this time, they were ineffective. Buddy's condition worsened. The large mass of scar tissue, remnants of the original abscess, became infected. I flew him back to Denver, where Jerry prescribed additional antibiotics, inserted surgical drains, and showed me how to administer a medicated wound flush. I couldn't help noticing that the vet's generally optimistic demeanor was absent.

Michael Stein

Once we were home again, it was apparent that Buddy's bunny friends were stressed and worried about him. Monique was especially anxious to groom and help care for Buddy. She didn't like the surgical drains protruding from his jaw and started jerking on them, trying to remove them. I had to isolate Buddy from his best friends.

The infection continued unabated. I hand-fed Buddy and gave him the medications, but nothing was working.

He's going to live. I wanted to believe but was having a hard time keeping my worries at bay.

We took another trip to Denver. Jerry surgically removed more of the disintegrated tissue, inserted new drains, and gave me instructions to flush the surgical drains every four hours. The only way I could do that was to take Buddy to work with me. He became my jump-seat passenger, accumulating more than 30,000 miles and becoming a frequent flyer!

The infection was finally contained, and Buddy slowly began to gain weight.

I quietly but joyfully plucked some tunes on my banjo, creating melodies that fit the rhythm and rhyme of "If wishes were horses."

After six weeks, the drains were removed. Even though the resulting holes had to be flushed, we were making progress. I happily shared the news with furred and non-furred family and friends.

After eight weeks, Jerry advised that flushes be done every six hours, rather than every four. A couple of weeks later, that was changed to every eight hours.

I will never forget the sound of Jerry's voice when he checked Buddy after that long three-month ordeal. He was optimistic again; I could hear his satisfaction over the phone.

Buddy is going to live! I was ecstatic.

So were his friends. They impatiently waited for me to set Buddy on the floor so they could welcome him back to the group. Their esteemed leader had returned.

For the first time in months, I really slept.

The specter of death vanished. The infection, bad as it was, seemed a blessing of sorts. It "ate" all the fibrous tissue in Buddy's jaw and the mass disappeared. Buddy is in better condition now than he has been in years: he weighs nine pounds, has returned to his avid explorations, and participates in everything!

"Hey, Buddy, let's go." As soon as I say the words, he is right there with me, friends trailing behind.

When I constructed a small waterfall in the yard of our new home, Buddy pranced in and out of the pit, then decided to direct my work and sunbathe from atop the short mud hill. "Muddy Buddy" was his nickname for a few days, but he was a happy rabbit and obligingly sat through the several brushings required to get his coat white again.

In addition to our more active pursuits, he and I enjoy sitting in the stillness of the night. With fewer distractions of civilization, we experience the quiet and settle into the rhythm of everything around us. At times like that I muse about the importance of protecting all living things. As we stargaze I tell him about Pegasus, the mythological winged horse who, for some, is a symbol of the soul journey, inspiration, and wisdom. Sometimes I tell Buddy stories about canoeing by starlight. Nighttime is the serene backdrop to our daily life.

Buddy seems to cherish our special times together. He embodies kindness and goodness—a fact I find amazing, considering all he's been through.

His cluster of rabbit comrades has grown to thirteen now and, although not the largest bunny in the group, Buddy remains the acknowledged leader. Each time I introduce a newcomer, Buddy courteously extends his nose in greeting, shows the new rabbit all the best places in the house and yard, and then lays out the rules for peaceful coexistence.

Maggie-dog continues to watch over the rabbits, and since Buddy thinks Maggie is wonderful, all the other rabbits love her too. "Outside!" brings the fourteen single-file to the door. Buddy follows Maggie, Colin follows Buddy, and the rest, including Monique and me, line up behind.

When it's time to come back in, the reminder "Home!" generally results in the group lining up single-file again. The sight never fails to make me laugh.

Whenever anyone asks me about rabbits, I talk about Buddy because his story is so incredible. What started as a sad commentary on human nature turned into a wonderful example of people working together to save one small rabbit and make this world a nicer place. Somehow, Buddy made his miraculous escape. Then a kind-hearted person took action, and that single phone call started a chain of events that saved Buddy's life.

When I tell the tale to his rabbit friends, Buddy sits on my lap, licking my hand when I get to the good parts, cuddling closer when I talk about the bad. My favorite part is telling how Pegasus, the winged horse, came to Buddy's aid:

. . . And then the brave white rabbit hopped onto the back
of his winged steed named Pegasus
and began his search for purest treasures:
love and joy.
His valor served him well as he determinedly
made the long voyage home.

The other rabbits appear to listen as I extol the bravery and resolve of their intrepid leader, the valiant voyager who never gave up his search for kindness and love, who never gave up his search for home.

ABOUT RABBITS: their social nature (and binkies)

Rabbits are exceptionally social creatures, expressing friendship and love in joyous and heart-warming ways. They groom, snuggle, play, comfort, teach, and cherish one another. It really doesn't matter what breed, size, or gender the rabbits are—their personalities will determine the level of friendship. A rabbit may even choose a companion of another species. Having a furred friend will help a sick bunny fight to survive and will often make the difference between life and death.

When a rabbit is already bonded with a human, it is not uncommon for the person to fear that introducing a second rabbit will diminish the affection the original rabbit has for his human companion. This is an unnecessary concern since rabbits are, by instinct, group animals and able to share affection with a number of friends. However, to remain on the rabbit's list of favorite companions, the human must regularly take the initiative to spend quality time with the bunny, during a time when the rabbit is receptive.

Rabbits thrive with love, companionship, and freedom! The more time that bunnies spend with their family and exploring the household environment, the more these sociable creatures become integral members of the family.

~

A bunny "binky" is a mid-air acrobatic feat. It's an expression of delight, a movement that demonstrates a rabbit's love of freedom and life. Each rabbit "binkies" in a unique way. A sideways jump, coupled with an air-spin. Ballet-like movements. A twist, twirl, and turn in mid-air. People have described binkies in many ways, all trying to capture the essence of the activity. A frolic in space. A small explosion of ecstasy. A wiggle of delight in flight. An expression of pure love and joy in the moment.

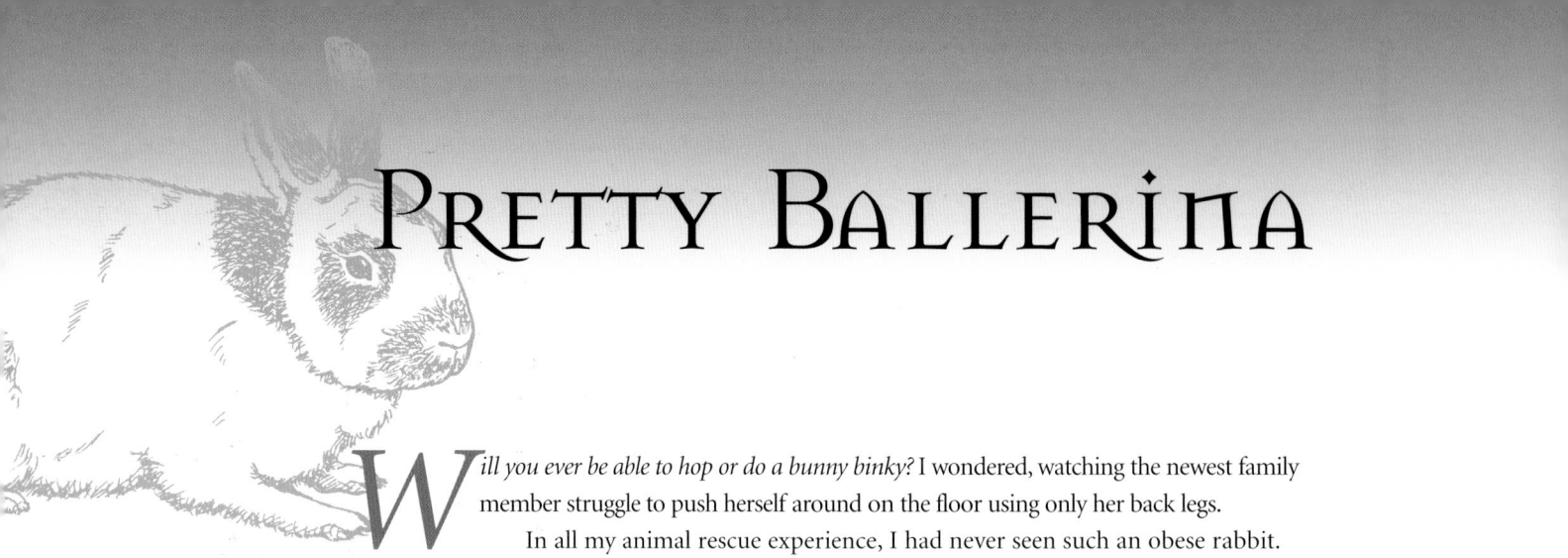

Pretty Ballerina

Will you ever be able to hop or do a bunny binky? I wondered, watching the newest family member struggle to push herself around on the floor using only her back legs.

In all my animal rescue experience, I had never seen such an obese rabbit. She had been abandoned in a cat carrier on my driveway earlier that week. I had rescued overweight rabbits before, but none in her condition.

Looking through the top grate of the carrier, I had been aghast to see a mostly black rabbit with large clumps of fur missing from her body and sores riddling her back. If the lesions were caused by fur mites, I knew that additional sores would likely be on her underside.

The rabbit was lying stretched out on a towel. It looked as though she was too heavy to stand, which meant she was lying in her wastes and probably suffering from urine burn. Her breathing was labored and ragged, too loud for me to hear if there were also any unusual gut sounds.

My original plans for the day were forgotten as I hoisted the carrier into the van. Calling ahead, I alerted the staff at the veterinary hospital that I would soon be arriving with a rabbit who needed emergency care.

The exam confirmed that the rabbit was a female, so grossly obese that she could not move. She weighed more than twice what she should have: instead of a svelte four pounds, she was nearly nine. As I feared, fur mites had eaten into her skin. Her back legs and belly were blistered and raw due to urine scald, and feces matted the fur remaining on her abdomen. The bunny was pale around her eyes and gums, her temperature was low, there were no gut sounds, and she had an acute respiratory infection.

I watched as the rabbit was stabilized, cleaned, and treated with fluids and medication. Then I held her in a towel containing a soft warming bag to help maintain her body temperature. The rabbit's dark eyes were dull; she lay too quietly.

Sharon Barrett Kennedy

"What name do you want for the records?" the technician asked.

I didn't have to think; her name immediately came to me.

"Ballerina. Her name is Ballerina."

I ignored the tech's expression, his eyebrow raised at the irony. In my mind's eye, I saw the lithe, graceful creature that Ballerina could become if she survived.

Once home, I followed the treatment plan prescribed by the vet, grateful that my office was only a room away. Ballerina required hydration, ointment, and medications, administered at regular intervals during the day. She needed to be cleaned frequently, but she disliked being held and it was awkward holding on to her round shape as she struggled. Afraid of injuring or dropping her, I made towel slings for lifting and turning her over.

As she grew healthier, I instituted the second component of the homecare regimen, designed to help Ballerina lose weight as well as regain health: an appropriate diet, with an emphasis on grass hay. But she showed not the slightest interest in the hay portion and ate none of it. Next, I tried tempting her with a selection of fresh cooking herbs, cut from my potted plants; she acted as though she hadn't the slightest idea what to do with them. I was relieved to see that she liked pellets, but she would eat only those that appealed to her—she left the grass-hay-based ones in the bowl.

Changing her diet was going to be a challenge, one that would probably continue for months. The weight loss needed to happen very slowly or Ballerina would be in danger of developing hepatic lipidosis, a life-threatening disease.

Incremental improvements marked the passing of time. There was the day Ballerina discovered she enjoyed watercress—from then on, she eagerly consumed leafy green vegetables. Not long after that, her pellet ration became solely timothy-grass-based.

"Good girl, Ballerina!" I declared as I stroked her.

However, my attempts to introduce hay into Ballerina's diet failed. She snubbed each type I offered, even after I added a sprinkling of dried herbs to make it more enticing.

A turning point in her physical activity came the day that Ballerina finally hopped! Not a very big hop, as she was still too heavy to get far off the floor, but hop she did. From then on, she began investigating her surroundings.

She looked kind of odd when she moved: instead of her back legs being positioned nicely under her body, they were spread wide to balance her weight. She did not look very rabbit-like as she waddled about, unable to sustain extended hopping. But that didn't stop her. She went from room to room, exploring—perhaps for the first time in her life.

Ballerina *loved* moving around! Eyes bright, it seemed she wanted to see and smell everything.

But it was almost a full year after her arrival before Ballerina impulsively began browsing on hay. As soon as she was eating a truly well-balanced rabbit diet, she began to have more energy. She was not only happier, but the good diet and exercise supported her weight loss. Over time, she took on the appearance of a normal, healthy rabbit.

During the evenings, I often listened to classical music for its calming effects. It was during Tchaikovsky's *Nutcracker Suite* that Ballerina lived up to her name and performed her first recital.

She gracefully entered the room to begin her *pas seul*—her solo ballet—bunny style. She leaped, beating her back legs together before landing, a perfect *entrechat.* Another leap, seemingly suspended in midair and ending with a small half-turn. Then she did a pirouette, performing the full-turn in the air rather than on her toes. Another graceful landing followed by a *glissade*, but rather than bringing her feet together after the glide, Ballerina ended her recital with another leap, followed by a twist and then a back kick.

"Ballerina! Pretty dancer!" I exclaimed.

She seemed synchronized with the music, or maybe that was just my imagination. A huge smile creased my face as I watched Ballerina combine fluid moves with energetic binkies. She was clearly enjoying herself, looking at me when I clapped and cheered. How good she obviously felt!

From then on, Ballerina performed bunny binkies, hops, jumps, and an occasional repeat of her dance solo. The latter always seemed to happen when I was listening to ballet music—she would hop first into the kitchen, then make a grand entrance into the living room, knowing that she had my full attention.

No longer the damaged, overweight, lethargic bunny of before, she had returned to the beauty and grace that was her birthright. A pretty Ballerina.

ABOUT RABBITS: issues of overweight

An *overweight* rabbit is heavier than his or her ideal weight, while an *obese* rabbit is at the high end of the overweight scale. Excessive weight can hamper normal activities such as grooming and movement. An obese rabbit who is unable to hop around loses out on many things, including the fun of exploring and following that inquisitive nose.

Additional weight gain is also a concern because of its effect on health, including cardiovascular disease, arthritis, and pododermatitis (foot infection). An obese rabbit is at high risk for hepatic lipidosis, sometimes referred to as fatty liver due to the accumulation of excess fat in the organ. If an obese rabbit is put on a strict diet and loses weight too rapidly, he or she can become ill very quickly with this life-threatening disease.

The Hidey Box

Hope had such an angelic face that I made an assumption—an unjustified and illogical one—that she would be sweet and gentle. I also assumed that, since she was an elder bunny, she would be more mellow than a younger rabbit.

When I brought the two-and-a-half-pound rabbit home, Hope immediately revealed the opposite of my expectations: she was willful, determined, and short tempered. She would not eat grass hay. She did not like the food pellets. Though unafraid of the cats, she did not want them encroaching on her space and signaled her irritation by loudly stomping her hind foot on the oak floor. She disliked being petted—or even touched. Whenever I had to handle her, to groom or administer medication, she would growl deep in her throat and drum her front legs repeatedly against my chest.

In addition, Hope seemed to be a rabbit completely devoid of rabbit social skills, something I found out after she settled in.

I had decided to try bonding Hope with my gentle threesome: Kumar, Merlin, and Smudge. Before starting the befriending process, the four had lived in close proximity and were familiar with each other's smells. I was certain that the three sweet-tempered bunnies would readily accept Hope and that she would fit right in—another of my erroneous assumptions.

Hope, smaller than the others, went on the offense immediately. She lunged at Kumar and bit him, holding on tight, unrelenting. Though I quickly removed her, I felt terrible that Kumar had been attacked and was very thankful that he was uninjured.

Further attempts to bond Hope with other bunnies failed, so I decided to give her more time to adjust. In due course, she became calmer, began eating hay, eagerly munched leafy greens, and decided that grass-hay-based pellets weren't so bad after all. Each day she ran around the house, exercising enthusiastically. Her attitude was improving so rapidly that I felt it was again time to try pairing her with another rabbit.

B. Endsley

Before I could do that, however, things changed remarkably.

Hope always made a game of racing in and out of the cardboard boxes located in her favorite corner of the living room. The assorted boxes, cut with holes, were spaced apart, with a towel in the midst of them for her to lie on.

One day midmorning, Hope brought all the boxes together, aligning the holes so that she could enter and exit without showing herself. She pulled the towel inside the largest box and then pulled some hay inside as well. This was unusual behavior, but in all other ways Hope appeared fine so I felt it was best to respect her new box-home.

During the next day's chores, I exchanged a clean towel for the old one and removed the strands of uneaten hay. As I moved the boxes slightly to tidy up, she impatiently waited for me to finish and then rearranged the boxes to her liking.

Before going to sleep that night, I put my book aside and got up to make my usual final check on the household. Turning on the hallway light, I stifled a shriek.

There, not one inch from my toes, was the largest spider I had ever seen. The dark, long-legged crawler had frozen in position. I stepped back, then raced to the kitchen and grabbed the first plastic cup I could get my hands on, intending to transport the creature outside.

"Good, she's still there," I thought, moving in to cover the immobile spider with the cup.

Shockingly, the cup was too small! The opening was at least three inches wide but the spider was broader than that. Not wanting to injure her, I went to retrieve a giant plastic cup.

By the time I returned to the hallway, the spider had disappeared. I looked everywhere, to no avail.

Remembering why I had risen in the first place, I checked on the rabbits. They were either browsing hay or resting. The cats seemed content as well, which meant they had not caught sight of the spider or they would have given chase.

I decided to return to bed, albeit slightly uneasy that such a large spider was somewhere about. I smiled to myself, though, thinking of times past when I would have gone light-headed at the sight of even a tiny spider. Determined to master that debilitating fear, I had researched arachnids until I appreciated their benefit in keeping the insect population in check. Now I was able to coexist with them, though I did not like being surprised by one.

Over the next couple of days, Hope continued to make the box-castle her resting spot.

Three nights after first sighting the spider, pandemonium broke out after I had turned in for the night.

"What in the world—"

Heart pounding, I stumbled through the house, groggy with sleep. The lights exposed the large chocolate-brown spider in Hope's corner. Two cats were intent on catching the spider, but Hope charged, making them back away. My jaw dropped as I watched the fast-moving spider scurry inside a box, Hope following close after.

"No, I don't believe it."

I had never read about a rabbit and spider living together, though certainly I knew it could be possible. They just seemed such an unlikely pair.

I began to worry about what would happen if Hope were bitten.

Finding my identification book, the closest match I could make was the forest wolf spider, a night hunter that feeds on small insects. Since wooded foothills of the Blue Ridge Mountains surround my home, I guessed that the arachnid had been rousted from her normal habitat during recent heavy rains.

From my reading, it seemed unlikely that the spider could injure Hope. And the two had obviously formed an uncommon friendship.

"Well, Hope needs a buddy," I reminded myself, returning to bed.

My cleaning routine the next day had one goal: to find out if Wolf, as I now thought of her, was actually living with Hope. I tilted up each box so that I could see underneath. Hope did not like my intrusion one bit! Clamping her teeth on the edge of a box, she attempted to pull it back down into place, but not before I spied Wolf behind her. What a contrast they made: Hope, furry white with black eye rings, and Wolf, dark and multi-legged. As I gazed at them, Wolf edged closer to Hope, as though trying to hide behind her.

I set the box down again, letting the secretive pair rest in the private spot Hope had designed for them.

Not much time has passed since discovering Wolf in the house, and she and Hope continue to share space. Hope is diligent about keeping the spider safe from the cats, lunging at them whenever they get too close. When I happen to see Wolf, she scuttles into their box-house. While Wolf is here, I will respect Hope's allegiance and won't attempt bonding her with another rabbit.

Is it my imagination or is Hope becoming friendlier? She seems gentler and happier, binkying around the living room and inviting petting. Maybe what she needed was a distinct mission—defending her new friend—and the enjoyment of sharing her home with a very special spider.

ABOUT RABBITS: non-bunny companions

Domestic rabbits instinctively seek out companionship, although there are times when a particular rabbit seems unable to form a relationship with another of the household rabbits. With proper introductions (monitored for safety and well-being), most rabbits live comfortably with a single companion or in a group. It's wonderful when a rabbit bonds with another bunny so that they can groom, cuddle, and nurture each other.

Whether or not they have a rabbit companion, the temperament of most bunnies allows them to lovingly bond with humans, and some will form relationships with the family cat, dog, and/or guinea pig (cavy). Rabbits may form a friendship with a bird, although some large birds (e.g., parrot family) can be aggressive toward bunnies.

Be aware that the presence of ferrets can be very stressful for rabbits. A ferret's method of play is very rough-and-tumble; because their skin is quite thick, ferrets playing together are generally unscathed. However, their play can easily kill a bunny.

When encouraging interspecies companionship, the human guardian must be mindful of the rabbit's prey status, confirm temperamental compatibility between the members, make careful introductions, and provide adequate supervision.

Bunny's Christmas Kingdom: Joy Uncaged

Information for this story was provided by Kimberly K. Dezelon

"Dashing through the snow
in a one-horse open sleigh;
O'er the fields we go,
laughing all the way. . ."

The merry sounds of the holiday classic matched my festive mood, interweaving with the scent of cinnamon as my husband, Michael, warmed nut rolls in the kitchen.

Our living room, rearranged to accommodate the decorated tree, provided the perfect setting for a lazy Christmas afternoon. I lay on the carpet, imagining what it would be like to see snow blanketing the city. But living in Phoenix, the only thing that would make our Christmas white was our precious mini lop, Bunny.

He must have known I was thinking about him, for all at once his full six pounds landed gently on my back. He crept to my shoulder, nuzzling through my long hair until his soft nose found my cheek.

Hi! His eyes—the rich brown of maple syrup—sparkled in greeting when I turned to look at him.

His happy gaze reminded me of the first day I met him.

Our nine-year-old son, Brock, carried a plain cardboard box. "Surprise!" he and my husband said in unison as they opened the carton.

Out popped my birthday gift: an adorable, lop-eared white rabbit.

Already acquainted with Michael and Brock, Bunny was more comfortable than most rabbits would be in an unfamiliar situation. His bright eyes assessed his new surroundings, including me. Then he bounded over to say hello and nudged against my hand, asking to be petted. My heart was captured instantly.

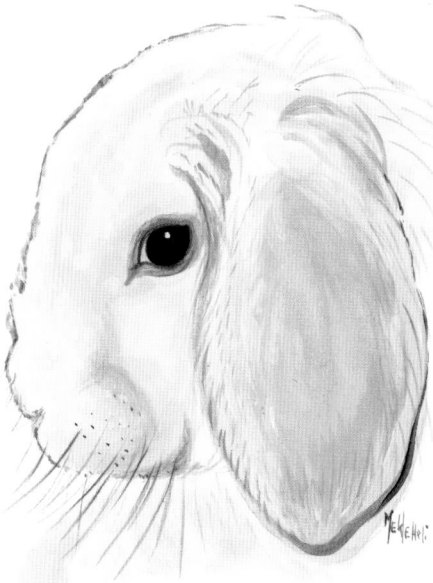

Bunny sprang off my shoulder, jarring me out of my reverie. He navigated the room in short sprints, making sudden stops to examine items that caught his attention. He was our little explorer who loved to investigate; he was curious about *everything*! Only a week ago Bunny had "helped" me make gifts for the local rabbit rescue organization.

He promptly absconded with one of the small paper bags filled with grass hay and pierced with holes. After entertaining himself with the twine closure, he pushed his paper toy all around the room as he tried to access the hay inside. Finally, he impatiently chewed a larger hole—and sat, contentedly munching.

While he was occupied, I wrapped lightweight boxes, some containing a healthy goody. As anticipated, Bunny gave up eating hay and instead begged a treat. He then made off with the wrapping paper roll, butting it down the hall and abandoning it under the bed.

My thoughts were interrupted as Michael and Brock entered the room. After setting a plate of nut rolls and sliced cranberry bread on the coffee table, the two of them became engrossed in their new camera. Our dogs, Barkley and Sabrina, rousted themselves enough to sidle close to Michael, hoping he remembered to bring them a treat.

I munched a nut roll, idly watching Bunny. He was amusing himself with a twist of dazzling ribbon. I smiled, thinking about the night before: Christmas Eve.

It was just before midnight and all seemed still. I moved stealthily back and forth along the hallway, feeling very smug as I carted secret gifts to the tree. For once, my plan to exhaust our son had worked. He was sound asleep. So was my husband, Michael.

But not Bunny!

I saw a flash of white tail as he disappeared around the corner ahead of me. I entered the living room and burst out laughing. There he was, standing on his hind legs next to the Christmas tree, forepaws held sweetly in front of his chest. His sparkling brown eyes held an unmistakable message: You can't sneak anything past me!

I knelt down to arrange the gifts under the tree, but Bunny had other ideas. He bumped a bright red box out of my hand, herding it around until colorful curls of ribbon on a green parcel caught his eye. After investigating that, he nudged under a large soft package and peeked out at me, signaling his desire to play.

I stacked some gifts and made tunnels with others. Our excited Bunny performed binkies around the tree, jumped over his snoozing canine friends (who kept a sleepy eye on the merrymaking), dashed through the tunnels, then vaulted to the top of the tallest box, as if surveying his Christmas kingdom. The tree's tiny colored lights reflected in his eyes as he hopped from one gift to another.

When he tired, he crawled into my lap, snuggled close, and nuzzled my hand to say, "Thanks"—just has he had done the first day I met him.

I enjoyed a leisurely stretch on the carpet and then sat up, not wanting to drift into a doze. I'd been awake past midnight and had hoped my small "alarm clock," Bunny, would sleep a little later than usual. But of course he, Brock, and the dogs rose very early, eagerly anticipating the opening of Christmas gifts; the remnants of our joy-filled morning were still strewn around the tree.

Michael selected the music to accompany our gift opening. The enduring English carol, "We Wish You a Merry Christmas," was the cue for our fun to begin.

"Good tidings to you
wherever you are,
Good tidings for Christmas
and a Happy New Year. . ."

As the words sounded softly in the background, I relaxed, content to watch my family open their gifts. While Barkley and Sabrina pawed their new fleece toys, Bunny tore his wrapped boxes apart, anxious for the papaya treats concealed inside. Then he joined in opening all the other gifts. He didn't care about the contents; he just wanted to play in the wrapping paper. As soon as there was an adequate pile, he began burrowing tunnels and bumping empty boxes into spots where they would provide the best cover. He cast aside the flat ones, trampled others in his exuberance, flipped paper wildly about, nosed over and under and through the lumpy, crinkly, multicolored mess.

Bunny enjoyed his splendid playground all morning. Finally, our darling little rabbit was so tired he simply fell asleep somewhere in the maze of his creation.

He was so entertaining, always totally immersing himself in family activities. Nothing I had read or heard about rabbits prepared me for the unexpected joy and hilarity that Bunny brought into our lives.

I got up off the floor, wanting a head start on packing for the trip to my parents' house in California. We planned to leave the next afternoon, as soon as the dogs' pet-sitter arrived. Bunny would go with us.

The little sweetheart was dozing on top of his bedraggled paper-bag toy. Much as I loved his antics, his "help" sometimes slowed completion of my tasks. I quietly headed to the bedroom, retrieved three suitcases and quickly packed Brock's.

I had almost finished my bag when Bunny appeared. Dashing through the doorway, he hopped onto a bedside stool and landed inside my travel bag, greeting it with unrestrained delight. He sniffed all the contents, proceeded to eject some, propelled others to one side, and then rearranged the rest. When my case was repacked to his liking, Bunny settled into it. He knew something wonderful was going to happen, and he wasn't going to miss a minute of it.

I couldn't suppress my laughter—his energy and enjoyment of everything were infectious. I gave up all thoughts of packing in an organized, timely manner and worked around Bunny's clowning.

We left the next day, looking forward to a wonderful family visit. Bunny sat in his large travel carrier, nibbling hay. When we arrived, he was somewhat hesitant to explore the new surroundings, but finally his curiosity got the best of him and he romped around the tree, repositioning and prodding packages into place. When he was satisfied with the new arrangement, Bunny took a seat among the parcels and serenely observed the holiday festivities.

My parents arranged the gift opening for the following morning so we could pretend it was again Christmas Day. It seemed I had slept only a short time when I was roused with a jolt; there was Bunny. When he saw I was awake, he hopped onto Michael's chest and nudged his chin. The eager rabbit waited until we were up, then jumped off the bed and disappeared through the open door.

Not wanting to disturb my parents, Michael and I quietly awakened Brock, and we tiptoed down the stairs.

"Dashing through the snow
in a one-horse open sleigh. . ."

The familiar music glided through the room. My parents were already up, watching our little white rabbit diligently investigating all the gifts. Bunny had amassed a group of packages and was singling others out; he looked like a busy little Christmas elf!

Brock and I lay down on the floor at Bunny's eye level. He took time away from his festal duties to hop over and gaze into our faces. His sparkling brown eyes held an unmistakable message.

What took you so long? IT'S CHRISTMAS!

Note from Brock Dezelon: "Dad and I surprised Mom when we brought Bunny home for her birthday. But Bunny surprised us all! He was so smart, quickly figuring out what we wanted and how to behave. We thought we'd have to train him, but we were the ones who really needed the training."

ABOUT RABBITS: holiday concerns

Holidays can be very difficult for household pets. The lack of normal routine, the visits from neighbors and relatives, the heightened excitement of children, and the frayed nerves of adults can seriously stress an animal to the point of illness.

During the holidays, it benefits a bunny (and other pets) to have quiet time, extra attention, and familiar routines as much as possible. It's also imperative to take protective measures for the safety and well-being of your animal companions. Cover or make inaccessible all electric cords. Do not let a bunny nibble on holiday plants, an artificial tree, or a cut or live tree treated with flame retardant, paint, or any other chemical. Prohibit access to water in the tree stand, and make holiday decorations (e.g., candles, tinsel, garland, breakable ornaments) inaccessible to prevent ingestion.

Wily, Rascally Dave

Information for this story was provided by Caroline Gilbert

"Now what's Dave up to?" I wonder aloud as I make my customary rounds of the outdoor rabbit sanctuary.

I can see the part-dwarf scamp cutting up and reckon he's intent on riling his neighbors, especially the other male rabbits. Dave seems to know more variations of how-may-I-provoke-thee than I can count.

Sure enough, as I draw near, I see the angelic-looking rascal goading the newcomer in an adjoining rabbitat. Dave races along his side of the enclosure, luring his next-door neighbor into following parallel to him. Then Dave reverses mid-stride and, before the other rabbit realizes what's happening, the rascal is flirting through the fence with the newcomer's mate. By the time the confused bunny figures out the strategy, Dave is innocently engaged in grooming rituals with Juneau, one of the two females who share his territory.

Dave's apparent guilelessness is a sham—black ears and nose keep close tabs on his opponent's position, but he deliberately sits facing away from the rabbit.

Since I have time, I decide to watch Dave's machinations for a while. He is a marvel of a rabbit and always makes me smile.

The white fur covering most of his body is thick and luxuriant—it practically shimmers in the bright sunlight. He looks so different from the first time I saw him.

In response to a call, I had gone to a local veterinary clinic. Dave was lying on a table, his almost-naked body wrinkled due to dehydration, bone-thin from starvation, and mite-infested. Classic signs of extreme neglect. The mites had feasted on Dave's poor body: a large scab covered his nose so he could not smell, and they'd eaten into his mouth, genitals, and feet.

"What on earth. . . ."

"He was kept in a small, stuffy glass aquarium in a school classroom," the vet told me. "The children were allowed to feed him whatever they wished."

At the end of the school year, the teacher sent the critically ill rabbit home with a student. Assuming by his appearance that the rabbit had a contagious disease, the child's mother wanted to get rid of him immediately. Another woman, looking for a companion for her rabbit, stopped by to meet the classroom bunny. She took one look, gathered up the frail body, and rushed him to the vet.

Caroline Gilbert

Instant countermeasures were started to try to save Dave's life: subcutaneous fluids, treatment for mites, special bunny food. After he was stabilized, the veterinarian called to ask if I had room for him at the Rabbit Sanctuary.

I remember feeling horrified at what this six-month-old bunny had gone through and heartsick that the children had witnessed it. The neglect, the lack of compassion—I couldn't stop thinking about what the children had inadvertently learned.

I brought Dave home and kept a close eye on him during the many weeks he needed intensive care. He was too weak to be anything but a model patient, but once in a while I saw signs of returning health: a nose twitching nonstop, ears rotating to follow sounds, and a growing appetite. Even more encouraging, I saw glimpses of his strong spirit.

My thoughts are suddenly interrupted as fun-loving, mischievous Dave begins to sashay around, rabbit style. In an instant, he becomes an acrobat: he flies through the air, jumps to the top of his house and down, and speeds around his province, circling his consorts, Millie and Juneau.

The two large, white New Zealand females are a good match for Dave. Tired of his antics, they corner him and demand attention. The three groom and cuddle together, nestling cheek-to-cheek.

It would be convenient for me to do some cleanup in the enclosure now, but I hesitate—it's still early. Better to wait until the sun is overhead and Dave is sleepy. Otherwise I'll have to contend with his wily schemes: his attempts to escape, to seek out new adventures, and to obstruct clean-up tasks.

I decide to return later and walk to the gate to say goodbye to this personable rabbit who is a favorite of many. The alacrity with which he runs to me is dizzying!

"Boy, I could use some of your energy!" I laughingly tell him.

Dave stands on his hind feet and lifts his black nose for petting. I affectionately stroke his ears and the area between his eyes, then softly massage his jaw. He closes his eyes in ecstasy. I can feel the rapid movement of his teeth; he's "purring," as rabbits do when they are happy.

Assuring him I'll be back, I give Dave a final caress, then watch as he exuberantly dashes to the center of his territory and leaps to the top of his house, keeping a sharp lookout for opportunities to bait, taunt, annoy.

I shake my head. What a wily, rascally rabbit!

ABOUT RABBITS: in a school classroom

Rabbits are generally not a good match for the classroom because the nature, requirements, and realities of rabbits, and those of children, are diametrically opposed. The match is good only if the teacher is unusually committed to making the experience as good for the rabbit as for the students. However, the various demands on a teacher's time often preclude that kind of commitment.

If someone wants to instruct children about rabbits, there are ways to develop intriguing lesson plans without having a rabbit live at the school. Bringing a cherished house rabbit to school for a short time one day allows the teacher, parent, or other adult to model respect and love for the bunny.

At the back of this book are two articles that discuss rabbits in classrooms. "Rabbits + Classrooms = *Mismatch*" outlines the many ways in which the needs of rabbits and children diverge. "Modeling Love and Respect for a Classroom Rabbit" provides information from a teacher about how to make a classroom experience fulfilling for both the rabbit and the children. Although this article is about a classroom, these ideas would also apply to a household with children.

Lobo and Blueberry

Dedicated to the memory of the Little Brown Rabbit

Information for this story was provided by Kay G. Fritzsche

"*MY BUNNY!*"

Five-year-old Alexa sobbed uncontrollably as she sat on the dusty ground. Her mother had taken the little brown rabbit and placed him where they had found him, huddled next to the petting zoo fence. Alexa did not want to leave the frightened, quivering little creature. She scooted across the dirt and put her arm protectively around the rabbit.

"*My* bunny," she softly whimpered.

It was hot—one of the dog days of summer. A too-hot-for-bare-feet kind of day. No breeze, not a cloud in the sky, sweltering. The little rabbit squeezed next to the fence, trying to find a tiny bit of shade and stay out of the way of other animals.

Alexa's parents felt sorry for the bunny at the petting zoo. It seemed dangerous for the small, defenseless creature to be penned with ostriches, goats, and a menagerie of other creatures. But it was time for the family to leave, and they didn't see an official with whom to discuss the rabbit.

Trying to explain to Alexa why she couldn't keep the rabbit proved useless. The young child cried all the way home and for days afterward talked about nothing but the little brown rabbit.

Alexa's mother, Kay, began reading books and searching the Internet for information about rabbits. The family's two large cats posed her greatest worry. After discussing her concerns with rabbit-knowledgeable people and receiving assurances that rabbits and cats often become friends, Kay and her husband surprised their daughter with a bunny for her birthday.

When Alexa saw the slate-blue, lop-eared bunny, she was ecstatic! But the three-month-old animal was frightened and cowered in his cage. He had been taken from his rabbit family and was now in a room full of strangers.

As she had done with the little brown rabbit at the petting zoo, Alexa gently stroked the bunny's ears and back. She soothed his fears and made sure the curious cats didn't get too close.

Within days the new family member was romping around the house. Alexa pranced after him and was quick to tell everyone, "He's *my* bunny."

Alexa named her little friend Blueberry and solemnly pledged to help take care of him. When Kay explained that rabbits can be injured if not held properly, Alexa agreed not to pick him up or carry him around the house. The very idea that her beautiful bunny could be hurt scared her. She promised to always sit on the floor before coaxing Blueberry to her lap.

But Alexa didn't forget about the little brown rabbit. She reminded her mother that he had been lonely and pleaded to return to the petting zoo to get him. If the brown bunny lived with them, she reasoned, Blueberry would have a playmate when she was at school.

Meanwhile, Blueberry demonstrated the same desire for a furry friend. With Alexa hovering protectively, he began circling Lobo, one of the family cats. The gentle giant watched with interest as Blueberry stopped in front of him, "presented" by lowering his head, and waited. Getting no response, Blueberry repeated his friendly rabbit routine, intent on establishing a bond with the big cat. But Lobo, puzzled by the lop-eared creature's behavior, simply watched, not understanding that Blueberry was asking to be groomed.

One day, Alexa hurried her mother into the foyer. There, sharing Lobo's favorite sun spot, the two animals slept side by side. Now, in addition to his doting human family, Blueberry had a furry buddy.

It was Blueberry who initiated the next level of friendship—he began grooming Lobo's large feet. When Blueberry lowered his head, Lobo responded with brotherly love and began licking behind Blueberry's ears. But the cat's raspy tongue tangled in the soft, downy fur, causing the floppy ears to bounce and flap wildly. Still, Lobo kept on licking, determined to be a good grooming partner.

Blueberry appreciated Lobo's efforts and reciprocated with gusto. He closely bonded with the big cat, followed him everywhere, and always slept with him.

The day old Lobo died, part of Blueberry died too. He was bereft without his best friend. No one—not even the family's new cat—could spark any interest in the despondent rabbit.

It seemed Blueberry would die of grief. With hope in their hearts, his family adopted a beautiful black rabbit from the House Rabbit Society. It was love at first sight! Blueberry didn't care that his new mate loathed cats. He didn't mind that she disliked the favorite place he had shared with Lobo. He eagerly welcomed Emma to his home, glad to finally be someone's hus-bun. Blueberry was in love and his life was complete.

Emma adored Blueberry, too. She demonstrated it, in part, by not allowing the family cats in the room she considered her and her mate's home. If one of the felines attempted to enter, Emma grunted and chased after the cat, intent on biting the intruder. As soon as the cat left the rabbits' room, Emma would race back to Blueberry's side and cuddle. The two became inseparable.

The family that had become "hooked on rabbits" celebrated! They toasted the love of Blueberry and Emma; they saluted the memories of Lobo and the little brown rabbit. When Alexa and her parents think back to the day they met him, their hearts ache. They keenly remember how frightened the beautiful brown bunny was whenever a larger animal came too close. They also remember how hot it was, but at the time they didn't realize that rabbits easily succumb to heat exhaustion.

But Alexa knows the little bunny is safe now. On a clear night she points to a special star. Whenever it appears to twinkle, she says it's the little brown rabbit doing a bunny binky. She knows he's never lonely or afraid anymore because there, in the star sparkling closest to him, is a constant companion: Lobo, the special cat who is a friend to all rabbits.

ABOUT RABBITS: children and bunnies

Adorable, fun, curious, comical, loving—most parents would use those words to describe their children. People who live with rabbits use the same words to describe their tiny dependents, so one might assume that children and rabbits are a good match.

The idea conjures a very sweet picture. But the picture is often incomplete, neglecting some of the sober realities of the situation. Children's time with bunnies must be closely supervised. Rabbits are stressed when harassed, become ill when fed unsuitable treats, and are easily injured when handled improperly (including being picked up by their ears).

Full responsibility for the family rabbit should be assumed by a parent or other adult; that is the only way that the wellbeing of both children and rabbits can be assured. Even if a child is unusually reliable for his or her age, the child should not be solely responsible for the rabbit's health and safety. Teaching children about bunnies begins with adults who are informed about proper rabbit care, consistently model the appropriate attitude and respect for the bunny, and set clear parameters to ensure the happiness, health, and safety of the rabbit. When grownups in the household model that kind of love and respect, everyone benefits.

Klezmer

Information for this story was provided by Caroline Gilbert

The white lop-eared rabbit was smaller than a tennis ball and weighed a mere ten ounces. She was tenaciously holding on to life, despite being starved, dehydrated, and ravaged by the parasitic disease, coccidiosis. Too weak to stand, the little one lay on her side, eyes closed.

I had been treating the bunny for eight days, but she didn't seem to be improving. She had arrived at the Rabbit Sanctuary as the only survivor of forty baby rabbits who had been given as carnival prizes. The children who had received them on that hot, humid South Carolina day had been so happy, thinking they would love and care for the tiny beings. Then the small rabbits began dying.

The families knew one another and shared what information they learned. It turned out that the diminutive bunnies had been taken from their mothers at about three weeks old, too early to survive without diligent care. Their living conditions at the carnival had been filthy and cramped. The summer weather—95% humidity and high temperatures—compounded the problem, since rabbits are very susceptible to heat exhaustion.

When news traveled through the community that the baby rabbits were dying, the parents of a young girl brought her tiny New Zealand mix to me, hoping I could save her life. Even though I had administered emergency measures, the young bunny remained in critical condition.

I looked down at the basket that held the small body, lying in a clean nest of warmed towels, and I wondered if she would live much longer.

During the ensuing days, I felt that my efforts might be futile. But then I entered the sanctuary's clinic one morning and Baby (as she was known) was sitting up in her basket! I was elated. For the first time, I dared to think that maybe, just maybe, she was going to recover.

I wanted to spend the morning with her, but there were many other rabbits to tend.

Andi Kleinman '08

Turning on the radio, I was delighted to hear the lively, cheerful sounds of klezmer music being played on a clarinet.

A movement caught my eye. Baby had wobbled out of her nest and sprung into the air! Then she leaped again, this time higher, and spun around. Baby was dancing in time to the happy tune, adding twists and turns. The intricate music sped up; she did too. But she was going too fast…the ball of white fluff collided with the wall. Not hard, but my heart leaped to my throat. Before I could get to her, Baby had rebounded to perform another flying jump, this time landing back in her basket. Exhausted, she lay there quietly.

I stood frozen in place amidst my chores, eyes wide with disbelief.

"Baby, that was amazing!"

A miracle, I thought to myself. *A miracle!*

From that moment on, the dainty lop made it clear that she was going to live life to the fullest—and I never again thought of her as Baby. To me, she became Klezmer.

Though she remained physically delicate and never gained all the weight she should have, Klezmer was a vivacious rabbit. I loved to watch her because she was so happy and upbeat, running instead of hopping. It seemed she added flourishes to every movement, performing graceful figure-eights in the air as easily as other rabbits hopped around.

I cherished the moments spent with her. When I entered the clinic, she'd run to me, asking for attention. When I held her, she would trustingly lean her soft body against mine. While I cared for the other bunnies, Klezmer would entertain all of us by racing and prancing around the room. Her pink eyes, eloquently expressing her zest for life, appeared to be bright with humor.

When healthy enough, she was paired with a handsome male Californian rabbit. The two lived in a shaded enclosure in a beautiful area of the sanctuary, where Klezmer continued to exhibit her high spirits—it seemed that she loved everything about life! Whenever I approached their territory, I could see her frisking about. When she spied me, she would immediately halt her gyrations, wanting to be petted.

Who would have guessed that a little carnival prize would survive such a difficult start and become a loving adult bunny? Klezmer was one of the lucky ones. She overcame her early ordeal, and her life continued to bring joy to many.

ABOUT RABBITS: carnivals & other public venues

In veterinary terms, rabbits are "exotics" and their constitution can be rather delicate. Those that are offered as "prizes" by carnivals and similar entertainment venues are usually adorable babies who are so young they cannot survive without special care. Unfortunately, most people do not have the specialized knowledge necessary to save the lives of such tiny, fragile beings.

Rabbits generally do not travel well, and illness can result from such stress. Proper care includes an appropriate diet, space to exercise, and clean living conditions—requirements that are often difficult for temporary setup or traveling groups. In addition, public settings often present stressors that trigger a bunny's fears and affect health. Mishandling—as well as the unfamiliar sounds, smells, and movements of both humans and other animals—can cause panic, injury, or illness in rabbits. While severe weather fluctuations may cause illness, untreated heat exhaustion can be rapidly fatal.

Finally, carnival-goers are awarded these living prizes whether or not they can provide a good home, know anything about caring for rabbits, or even want a bunny. The kindest solution is for carnivals and other entertainment venues to offer stuffed toy animal prizes, rather than the real thing.

The Rabbit Round-Up

Information for this story was provided by Caroline Gilbert

We sized each other up—

Four adult humans;
three adult rabbits.
Each of us tipped the scales at over one-hundred pounds;
each of them weighed less than ten pounds.
We were confident in our ability to rescue the rabbits;
the small creatures were not about to trust us.
We pondered our plan and strategy;
they were poised and ready to scatter.

The rabbits had been dumped on a farm owned by my neighbor, Ann.

It was early on a cool, crisp October day;
gold and red leaves contrasted against the clear blue sky.

It was time for the round-up to begin.

We started with the black-and-white rabbit who had wandered toward the cows. Cautiously, slowly, the four of us moved closer around him, creating a barrier between the large cattle and the small rabbit. We took our time, trying to give the impression that corralling a dark-eyed bunny was far from our intent.

As we got closer, we hunched and stooped, attempting to make ourselves look smaller, less threatening. Even though our slow pace increased the chances of rescue, it felt like we were dawdling the morning away.

The circle closed. Squinting against the bright sunlight, my son, Charley, and I got down on our knees, then on all fours.

"Get him!" We issued the order to one another, simultaneously springing forward in what we now boast was one well-coordinated maneuver. After grappling a bit, we stood like Siamese twins joined at the rabbit, proudly announcing the obvious: "We got him!"

After settling the black-and-white bunny into a crate, we decided to capture the white rabbit. He had other ideas and began exploring a new frontier thick with honeysuckle and prickly blackberry. We tagged behind. The rabbit hopped a bit, then sat. Hopped, sat. We advanced. Darn, too fast—a blur of white flashed away. We tarried; he slowed.

"Pretty boy, good boy," I murmured reassuringly. But as we moved deeper into underbrush, it morphed into a plea.

"Come here, bunny. Please, come."

Good fortune finally joined us, leading the rabbit into a natural basket of loosely tangled vines. My fellow rescuers gently pressed down on the snarled mass, blocking the rabbit's escape. I scooped him up and held him close, softly stroking his head to lull his fears.

We were riding high on confidence, but the third rabbit kicked it right out from under us—the brown-and-white Dutch ran clean away. We hated giving up the rescue attempt; that little Dutch bunny didn't stand a chance of surviving on his own. But it was getting late and had started to rain, and finding him in dense thicket would be impossible. Maybe tomorrow, I hoped.

Back at the Rabbit Sanctuary, I tended the two rabbits we had captured. The black-and-white buck was in terrible condition. Long crooked teeth pinned his mouth shut: top teeth had grown into the bottom jaw, bottom teeth speared the top. The ability to eat had been out of the question. Knowing the agony had to be nearly intolerable, I performed emergency procedures: administering pain medication and fluids and clipping his incisors. After making sure his temperature was stable, I syringe-fed small amounts of special mash and wondered if his bony body would survive the necessary tooth extractions.

The white bunny was more fortunate; he was immobilized with fear and much too thin, but there were no signs of serious health problems.

Too early the next morning my neighbor, Ann, called again. Instead of telling me she had found the brown-and-white Dutch, she starkly described a new rabbit: big, white.

No one else was available to help this time, so I hurried over alone. A terrified New Zealand rabbit led Ann and me on a roundabout. We soon admitted defeat, and Ann drove off to get help.

I perched on a boulder and watched the large, pink-eyed rabbit, who calmed now that I wasn't acting like a

O. Earl McCullough

predator. In due time, he appeared comfortable with the arrangement and began contently eating his way along the creekside. This was my chance to make him understand.

"Mr. Big," I called softly.

The rabbit sat straight up, ears erect. In a magical moment I clearly understood him: My friends and I were crowded together in a wire cage, hungry and miserable. We knew there was no hope for us. Then suddenly, we were thrown out. We were scared, but realized this was our chance. We were starting to enjoy our freedom when you—

"You don't stand a chance out here," I interrupted. "The white of your body makes you an easy target during the day; you glow in the light of the moon at night. I promise that you can live your dreams, but you've got to let me catch you."

I knew that made no sense to him. How would letting me catch him allow him to be free? Pink eyes flashing, he sprinted away. Naturally, I followed.

Just then, Ann returned with a young neighbor, home on military leave. We three hustled along the boggy bank of the creek. The rabbit split left; we tried to head him off. He panicked, reversed, raced up the steep ditch, and followed the roadway up a long incline.

"He's bound to tire soon," the young man said.

I couldn't respond; I was too busy huffing and puffing. That rabbit would tucker out eventually, but I was already tired! And worried. The rabbit was becoming stressed by our rescue attempts. Then a new thought entered: *what if a vehicle came barreling down that road?* My fears must have reached the vulnerable creature; just that quick he veered from the road and leaped down the ditch wall.

We wanted to keep him in our sights. The young man began running after him, then yelled back to me.

"There's a culvert! He ran right in!"

A culvert? What luck! The cadet raced to the far end just in time to see the rabbit burst out at top speed.

"There he goes!"

But hope was instantly reborn. Another of the concrete drains was sighted; the white streak was heading straight for it.

Ann and the military cadet set off for the far end of the culvert, while I followed big white rabbit feet into the narrow opening. I was immediately greeted by claustrophobia; it hugged me fiercely.

I couldn't breathe. The culvert was just slightly larger than I was. It looked very, very long. I closed my eyes for a second. When I opened them, the space seemed even more intimidating.

My heart gladdened to see the rabbit in there with me. He was a big-eared silhouette against the circle of light coming through the far end. Maybe he would let me catch him and back right out; it was a hopeful thought.

I stretched flat on my belly and began pulling myself along on my elbows. Progress seemed imperceptible. The rabbit hopped on ahead. Drat, he was going to make me go the full distance.

Inch by inch, I moved along. The skin on my elbows was raw and begging me to stop. I forced myself to visualize openness and sunlight as I continued to worm forward. Then the light went out; Ann and her young helper had closed off the escape.

The rabbit reached the end—no hops left. A while later I joined him—almost no breath left.

Whispering assurances that he would not be harmed, I elbowed myself still closer, trying to work up the nerve to reach out and clasp my hands around him. I hesitated. What if the terror-stricken rabbit considered my touch his doom? I shuddered to think he might emit that piercing, childlike scream, as rabbits often do in the throes of death.

"Please, please don't scream," I entreated.

Reaching forward, my hands firmly clutched his body.

He didn't scream. But he kicked and struggled until Ann and the young man reached in and lifted him from my grasp. After assisting me from the culvert, the two praised the rescue effort.

"Just like a scene from *Alice in Wonderland*," Ann said.

"A good military training exercise," the cadet enthused.

I didn't share their opinions. For me, it was a huge relief to be out of that suffocating space and to know the New Zealand rabbit was finally safe.

On the way home, I glanced at the huddled body on the seat beside me. The rabbit did not feel rescued any more than I felt like a rescuer. He looked as though his dreams of freedom had been crushed. I felt like a monster. This would not do.

"You would not have made it on your own," I reasoned with him. "First of all, you are the wrong color; you cannot hide from your enemies. Second, you would have been doomed to starvation."

To keep my attention off my abraded, burning elbows, I told Culvert (it seemed the perfect name) about the good food he'd eat and play spaces he would share with a female bunny friend (after he was neutered, of course, but I did not mention that).

After a few weeks of getting used to his new surroundings at the sanctuary, Culvert settled in and established himself as king of his territory. His queen was a beautiful spotted female named Juniper Berry, who had been cruelly abandoned. The two companions played and dug, cuddled and slept.

Culvert didn't seem to miss his former buddies, but I made sure he knew they were safe and healthy, even the black-and-white rabbit. His front teeth had been removed, but he was doing just fine picking up food with his gums and chewing with his molars. All three of the male rabbits had kingdoms of their own. Never again would any of them see a wire cage.

Time passed peacefully and lazily for them. A year later, on a beautiful, clear autumn day—just like the day I first encountered the abandoned rabbits—I watched Culvert and Juniper Berry busily nibbling fallen leaves. They looked up when I called and happily ran to greet me.

Culvert's pink eyes glowed in the sunlight as he looked into mine. I'm sure I heard him say, My dreams have all come true.

ABOUT RABBITS: abandonment

Some people release pet rabbits into natural areas in the mistaken belief that liberation will allow the rabbits to revert to wild behavior and live freely. The reality is quite different. Because of selective breeding, domestic rabbits *cannot* survive in the wild.

True wild rabbits rely on speed and wariness to survive. Selective breeding, however, has modified such traits in the domestic bunny, creating animals who are more sedate and more trusting of humans and other predators. Many rabbits live with cats and dogs and do not fear them. Selective breeding has also created particular body configurations and distinctive coats that put domestic rabbits at a disadvantage in the natural world. For example, many rabbits have white in their coloring, making them visible even at night.

Even if rabbits are abandoned in an area with limited predators, they would not know the location of food and water sources and would die of starvation and dehydration. They will not form social bonds with wild rabbits nor will they be protected by their wild cousins.

The same holds true for bunnies released in an urban area. The fact remains that domestic rabbits have been bred to depend on human caregivers—they cannot survive on their own outside, no matter how lush the grass or how delectable the garden.

Turning a bunny loose to fend for himself is tantamount to the rabbit's death sentence. And a group of domestic rabbits fares no better.

Note: In this story, as well as in "The Valiant Voyager," rabbit-knowledgeable caregivers take emergency measures to save the rabbits' lives, including clipping the incisors. However, for a number of important reasons, treatment of dental problems generally should not be performed by non-professionals. Reference the article at the back of the book, "Rabbit Teeth: The Importance of Proper Care," by Dr. Angela Lennox.

The Priceless Tulip

In memory of Courtney McCarty Johnson, who provided information for this story

He was dying. I knew it as soon as I saw him. One of the other volunteers at our animal shelter quietly confided that three other bunnies had died soon after they were brought into our facility.

Carefully lifting the two-month-old bunny out of the cage, I held the tiny, furry dependent. He was puny, just fur stretched over a skeleton. Stitched wounds ran along his back; some brown hair was just beginning to grow around them.

I cleaned his soiled hindquarters, then situated the uncomplaining sweetheart in a towel-lined box and offered him enticing, hand-made whimsies. While he poked at the playthings, I scrubbed out and refilled his water and food containers.

Gently picking him up again, I nestled the small body in the curve of my jaw and neck. What a cuddly package of sweetness he was! He squirmed into a more comfortable position; his ears tickled my chin as I lightly rubbed his jaw and stroked his face.

He wiggled with pleasure, which delighted me too.

I contemplated returning him to his cage, but worries filled me. It would be two days before I could return. *Who would make sure he was properly fed? Who would administer the prescribed doses of medication at the right times? Would he have play time or remain in his cage all day, alone and depressed? How would he handle the continued stress of being housed in a room of cats meowing their misery?* If the bunny's needs were not met, he would die.

A staff member entered from the canine quarters, and the barking of eager dogs waiting to be adopted entered with him. The bunny flinched and tried to duck into the folds of my sweatshirt. That decided his fate: he was going home with me.

While completing adoption papers, I heard his story. Someone had discarded the baby rabbit in a garden after a dog attacked the tiny prey animal. An elderly man rescued the injured baby from a bed of tulips and rushed him to the Denver facility, where emergency veterinary treatment prevented the rabbit's death from shock.

After his wounds were cleaned and stitched, the little one was put into a cage in the only place available—a room filled with caged and distressed cats. After that the young bunny was basically ignored because staff members were unfamiliar with the temperament, behaviors, and needs of rabbits.

Courtney McCarty Johnson

Tulip, named for the flowers in which he had been found, was delighted to accompany me home. He was even more excited to find he was going to live with a playmate, Benjamin Bunny. The two became bonded buddies without delay.

Tulip, still a baby, was not exhibiting his full personality yet, but I blithely assumed he would be much like Benjamin Bunny, my "perfect little Dutch boy" who is sweet and quiet and prides himself on keeping his brown-and-white coat neatly groomed. Oh, how very wrong I was. And how illogical. Why would two distinct little beings have the same personality? Before long, Tulip began demonstrating his.

He nosed open the office door (I still do not know how he accomplished that) and chewed through the computer cables. Thankful the equipment was off and he had not been injured, I replaced cables and covered them with hard plastic conduit. Before I could complete the task, he had severed the telephone connection. Then the stereo wires.

When I saw him eyeing baseboards, I smugly stayed one hop ahead and sprayed them with bitter apple—only to learn the taste was much to his liking. I had to do some "creative" decorating, the looks of which would never pass a house-beautiful test!

After Tulip was neutered, he seemed to settle down, and I succumbed to a false confidence. Until it was time to clean bookshelves. Without a second thought, I laid some of the volumes on the coffee table. Tulip climbed aboard and chewed the edges of my most valued book, a sentimental gift. He snubbed the inexpensive paperbacks.

I was really exasperated and completely dumbfounded. The rabbits had a nice supply of hard plastic toys and unsprayed apple branches. Why wasn't Tulip chewing on those?

"Why can't you be more like Benjamin?" I heard myself grumble time and again.

My patience came to an end the day I heard a loud rip from behind the sofa. I ran over and looked behind it. There sat my dark-cheeked adolescent, covered with stuffing. He had the most innocent look on his little face, as if to say, "I don't know how this happened, Mom. That couch just blew this all over me!"

All my frustration and irritation came out in one vocal blast. Tulip's nut-brown eyes widened in fear, and he scurried to a hiding place.

I felt awful. I knew better than to yell at any animal, especially one as sensitive as a rabbit. But what was I going to do with Tulip? His ripping and gnawing were emptying my bank account. I was beginning to call him Pricey Tulip!

Then it hit me. The all-important rule when bringing a rabbit into one's home is *think like the rabbit.* Instead of "listening" to Tulip's needs through observation and analysis of his behaviors, I had assumed he would outgrow his chewing habits and become like Benjamin Bunny. Not only did Tulip have the attribute of youth, which made him naturally a bit wild and unruly, but he had been striving to gain my attention in order to say he was *B O R E D*!

With my new awareness, I began shopping—bunny style. Within hours of returning home, the family room was transformed into a rabbit paradise. Cardboard tubes edged the sides of the couch. Boxes of various sizes and shapes, each with escape holes and all sturdy enough to jump on, added interest. The *pièce de résistance* was a plastic playset that had inclines and platforms. Secret passageways and a courtyard completed the rabbit kingdom.

Tulip did not wait for me to finish. He immediately entered the tubes, his best friend close behind, and a spirited game of chase began. The two agile racers maneuvered the course, jumping and short-cutting their way around as they explored the new territory.

In a surprise move, Tulip ran over to me, jumped into my lap, and reached up to lick my face. A quick "thank you" (something he had never done before), a brief rest, and he was off again.

Tulip has taught me well. Even though our rooms are completely bunny-proofed, I do not leave him to roam the house unattended. He is a rabbit who lives in anticipation of new adventures and challenges. And as I continue to think like a rabbit, I am able to meet those challenges.

Tulip seems content with his life now. He and his buddy, Benjamin Bunny, have plenty of safe chewable objects, and I reconfigure the play spaces often enough to keep their interest piqued.

I am content now too. I have happy, healthy bunnies—a source of great joy. I have Tulip to thank for that. Precious and priceless, that's my Tulip!

ABOUT RABBITS: bunny-proofing the house

Rabbits present some unexpected challenges, especially when it comes to their natural instincts to chew and dig. Sometimes it may seem that nothing is safe from a rabbit's teeth or that he will dig right through the floor!

To prevent injury or death to the rabbit and damage to the household, bunny-proofing is essential. Since chewing and digging are strong instinctive behaviors, make tempting objects and spaces inaccessible, use deterrents, and furnish appealing alternatives. Also keep in mind the social nature of rabbits and provide ample companionship and play.

Effective bunny-proofing requires a proactive state of mind. To stay at least one hop ahead, get down on the floor, survey your rabbit's world, and start thinking like a rabbit!

Note: Information on bunny-proofing is readily available from rabbit rescue organizations and other sources, including a chapter in Marinell Harriman's House Rabbit Handbook.

Brown Beauty

Information for this story was provided by R. Lee Terence

Some say Show Low, which acquired its name from the winning hand in a poker game, is simply a small rural community. Others say it's a vacation destination. One thing is certain: Show Low's location at the edge of the Mogollon Rim ranks it with some of the prettiest places in all of Arizona. But, as can happen anywhere on this old planet of ours, some days that beauty is marred, as it was one cold, gray, drizzly day in April.

Parking at a street corner, a man unloaded several boxes and placed them under the ponderosa pines. He opened them, then climbed back into his vehicle and drove off.

A concerned neighbor who observed the incident was the first to call. "Bunnies are running all over the place! Could be a dozen. Maybe more."

I didn't ask for many details. Frankly, I long ago passed needing to know the particulars. After years of working with organizations that rescue cats, dogs, horses, birds, and any other unfortunate animal that is abandoned, neglected, or abused, I've seen more than I ever wanted to see of what some call the dark side of human nature.

Domestic rabbits running loose could mean only one thing: someone had abandoned them.

I loaded the humane traps and sped along the highway. Two kind-hearted citizens anticipated my arrival and were waiting; they began talking before I got out of my truck.

"Roaming dogs got two of 'em!"

"One got hit by a car."

By this time, the bunnies, crazed with fear, had scattered. I looked around, noting the fact that the man who dumped them had chosen an area that had a bit of underbrush, an overturned boat or two, and some resident vehicles. At least the defenseless animals had a few places to hide.

I had to hurry; frenzied barking meant the dogs had probably killed a third. The two compassionate residents helped me set up live-catch traps, and from then on, it was a waiting game.

Turns out we didn't have to wait long: two emaciated rabbits bolted eagerly into traps to devour the cilantro. Two, then four, were moved to safety. A couple of hours passed; we captured another, and then my helpers had to head for home.

I was alone, and patience and worry sat side-by-side on my shoulders. The clouded sun was setting, and the tall pines made nightfall even darker.

I was sure two bunnies were still alive. Thinking parsley might tempt them, I used some to bait the traps, all the while keeping an eye on the dogs eagerly scouting the area. I was luckier than the dogs; hunger finally got the best of both rabbits and they willingly allowed themselves to be snagged.

While transferring the last rabbits to carriers, I spotted a skinny, unkempt, brownish-colored bunny watching from the sidelines. It looked as if she might be injured.

I readied a trap and stationed myself to watch. The scrawny rabbit's swift motion took me by surprise: she raced in, snatched the offered fare, turned tail, and disappeared! I arranged more tempting sprigs, this time further back. The same thing happened. She was hurt but smart; she'd figured out how to pull out the food without engaging the trap door.

Cold as it was, I was determined to get this plain little girl, whom most would overlook in favor of some exotic-looking rabbit. I just hoped I could catch her before some predator did.

But my luck ran out. Daylight disappeared, the rabbit along with it. It was almost inky out there; the clouds had settled low, cloaking the tops of the ponderosas. I knew better than to use one of my high-powered flashlights—that would've done more harm than good.

I hoped the bunny was in hiding and sent a mental message that she should stay put. Fastening a big bundle of greens as far back as possible, I made sure she'd have to really work to get any, then covered the trap with my heavy canvas tarp and secured everything tight against the wind. A flapping, noisy thing would certainly scare that rabbit away.

When it was obvious there was nothing more I could do, I sent out a little prayer and went home.

Just after dawn, I checked the trap. There she was, sitting inside, her stand-up ears perked forward, with a look that said, "WHAT TOOK YOU SO LONG?"

The dingy-brown bunny obligingly let me put her in a carrier. Once home, the amiable little one let me inspect her dog bites and care for the wounds. Then she ate her first nourishing meal in a long while, maybe the first one ever. She was so unbelievably thin; the sparse coat of dirty fur couldn't hide the sharp feel of her backbone or the obvious edges of her ribs. There were scrapes and tears in her skin. She wouldn't have lived much longer.

The veterinarian guessed the rabbit was just over a year old. She weighed four pounds, about half what she should have. As soon as she was healthy enough, I was going to have her spayed by a vet who was skilled in treating rabbits. I'd already contacted Brambley Hedge Rabbit Rescue about that.

Brown Beauty is what I called her, Beauty for short. I thought it was a fitting name for a rabbit who had an inner strength and sweetness that surpassed many of my acquaintance. She was outgoing, yet gentle. And she didn't mind being picked up, an unusual trait in most rabbits, but especially amazing in one so obviously neglected. As Beauty regained strength and her wounds began to heal, she started running around the house and had a grand time finding out-of-the-way places to hide. She was always glad to see me, though, and would come when called.

Three weeks after she was trapped, just before she was to be spayed, Beauty began stuffing her mouth with impossible amounts of hay and frantically racing around the living room. She emptied the contents of her mouth and worked that hay around with her nose, then grabbed it up and ran to another place.

I'd never seen anything like this before. A call to Brambley Hedge brought me up short: Beauty was trying to find a place to build a nest! She was such a skinny little thing that I hadn't considered that she might've been pregnant when I trapped her. I wondered if it could be a false pregnancy. I hoped so, but wasn't going to bet on it.

Well, if Brown Beauty was going to deliver, she'd need a cozy box. I gave her one I thought would work. Sure enough, she finally decided that was where she'd build the nest. After forming a circular depression in the hay, Beauty pulled fur from her breast and made a warm, downy bed for her babies. I'd found out that when a doe is about to deliver, the fur on her chest loosens, providing soft nesting material and exposing her nipples for nursing.

After all that, Beauty lay quietly, as if tired by her work. Just before bed, I peeked in on her; she was squatting over the nest. Worried that she might leave droppings there, I stuck around to clean up. But a short time later, when Beauty eased herself away, there were two tiny pink babies. Five more followed. A couple of days later, enough fur had grown on their naked bodies for me to see their individual colors: black, gray, tan, brown, and one blond runt.

After what Beauty had endured, it seemed miraculous she could deliver seven perfect babies.

In typical human fashion, I accepted the miracle, then started worrying. *Would Beauty be able to care for her tiny, blind dependents? What if she was too stressed to produce milk? What if she deserted them?*

B. Ondsley

At first, I thought my fears had been realized. Beauty covered her brood with fur and hay, hopped away, and lay down as far from them as she could get. I moved her close to her kits, hoping she'd take an interest in them, but she snorted and returned to where she had been. Finally, I called Brambley Hedge again and learned that mother rabbits stay away from their odorless babies so as not to attract predators. I was assured that Beauty most likely would take care of her babies during the night; I sure hoped so. It was a long, fitful night for me.

The next morning, there she was, just where I had left her the night before. I lifted a bit of hay and fur off the nest and was relieved to find all the babies had round little bellies and unwrinkled skin. They'd been fed.

For days, I never saw Beauty approach her offspring, but they were always clean and well fed when I peered in on them.

It occurred to me what a privilege it was to observe Beauty, one of the prettiest rabbits around, exhibiting such pure love. Confidently and single-mindedly, she gave herself to her little ones. In her sweet, unassuming way, she nurtured her babies, treating them all as the perfect little beings they were. To me, that's beauty by any name.

ABOUT RABBITS: benefits of spaying and neutering

It is obvious that spaying and neutering reduce rabbit overpopulation and its resulting horrors (neglect, abandonment, and euthanasia). Less well known, perhaps, is the fact that "fixing" also helps to:

- more readily accomplish litter box training
- reduce hormonally driven aggression and grouchiness
- eliminate territorial spraying
- decrease the chances of a female rabbit's dying of uterine or mammary gland cancer.

For the comfort, health, and well-being of your rabbits, have them spayed or neutered by a veterinarian experienced in treating rabbits. Most vets prefer to spay a healthy female when she is between 4 and 6 months of age. Performing a good spay before that age is technically difficult and may result in retained tissue, which can produce hormones throughout the rabbit's life and result in behavior problems.

Healthy male rabbits can be neutered after their testicles descend. The testicles of small and average-size males may drop down as early as 10 weeks of age and almost always by the age of 3-1/2 months, while the testicles of giant breeds may not be evident until the age of 8 months.

Human guardians should become aware of the factors and variables that affect sexual maturity, separating male and female bunnies at the appropriate age to prevent unwanted litters.

Ramona

Information for this story was provided by Ingrid Harding Irvine and Dr. Peg Frank

"She's not a very nice rabbit," said the nature center employee. "When kids visit, she always lunges and tries to bite."

It was the end of October—a beautiful Indian summer day in Minnesota. Ever since I was a kid, I have loved the sound of leaves crackling underfoot, and today was no different. I could have stayed outside all day. Too soon, the rabbit building came into view. . . nothing more than a chicken coop.

As the employee opened the door, I was greeted by stench. Mice and chickens scurried out of our way as I was shown the Florida white rabbit I had come to pick up. There were maggots in her food, the drinking water was nearly as dirty as she was, and the only place for her to sit was on a thick layer of feces.

Looking around, I saw two other rabbits who fared just as poorly. Now I understood why concerned individuals had asked the Minnesota Companion Rabbit Society to help improve care of the rabbits. I was one of the members coming to help.

The center was grateful for our assistance in taking the rabbits for veterinary care, including neutering. The Florida white, at least four years old, had badly misaligned teeth. After she was spayed and her teeth filed to normal shape, I took her home for aftercare. When recovered, she would be returned to the nature center, which had agreed to improve conditions: new cages, appropriate food, and better public education about rabbit care.

Before those changes were made, however, the center administrators made the decision to relinquish two of the three rabbits. The Florida white became my foster bunny and, oh, what a feisty one she was, earning her the name Ramona, after the spunky little girl in the children's book series.

Ramona wasted no time in demonstrating her well-defined boundaries—and insisting they be respected! She was four pounds of fierce determination, flattening her short ears, growling deep in her throat, and lunging whenever anyone got too close. I guessed that she had developed this survival strategy as protection against visitors at the nature center.

Ingrid Harding Irvine

She settled in quickly, exhibiting tidy household habits and choosing the living room as her personal quarters. For weeks, I spent periods of time near her on the floor, signaling that she could trust me. Though she eventually stopped lunging at me, she disliked being held, even on my lap. I was delighted when she finally let me caress her favorite spot: her cute white nose. When I would stop stroking, she would nuzzle her face into my hands, asking for more of the gentle touches.

We developed a strong bond, this little short-bodied rabbit and I. Ramona was so clear, so unambiguous. Despite her generally spirited nature, she always seemed pleased to see me. She was secure in who she was, independent, and willing to love and be loved. I cherished her and was happy that she was part of my life.

At regular intervals, Ramona went to the animal clinic for teeth filing. It was during one of those routine visits, on a sunny day in June, that Dr. Peg found the first lump. It was small, about the size of a BB. The biopsy results were not immediately available, but they ultimately revealed mammary adenocarcinoma, cancer of the mammary glands. I listened with a sinking heart as the vet explained the seriousness of the disease.

"The mortality risk is quite high with this type of cancer because there is only a small window of opportunity to treat it," Dr. Peg said. "It spreads throughout the body by traveling through the lymphatic system, including to the brain and nervous system."

I was stunned; Ramona seemed so healthy and happy. I wanted to know everything about her chances.

"Right now she seems fine, and that's usually the way it is at first." The sympathy in Dr. Peg's voice was evident as she further explained the disease. Her voice softened when she verified my fear, "The long-term prognosis for Ramona is not very good."

Tears filled my eyes. It didn't seem fair for this rabbit, who had so recently gained a better life, to suffer from such a severe disease.

The weight of the diagnosis shattered what was supposed to be a time of celebration: Ramona was soon to be adopted by a loving family. Though I was saddened to think she would not share my home anymore, I had been happy that she was going to a permanent home. But what would happen now?

Ramona's new family listened as I told them the news. After honest discussion, they realized they would not be able to provide the medical care she needed. Because it was unlikely that another family would want a rabbit with such serious health issues, I adopted Ramona.

She weathered the lumpectomy well, returning quickly to normal behaviors. She ate hay and fresh leafy greens with such gusto that I was hopeful Ramona would be the exception and that no additional lumps would form. That was not to be. I was the one who discovered the second lump just four months later. It was in a different teat, confirming that the cancer was spreading. Another lumpectomy was performed, with Ramona recovering almost overnight.

It was now November, and I was determined that the holidays would be filled with joy and love, not with worries about Ramona's future. I wanted her to experience life to the fullest—and I wanted to enjoy every moment of her presence that I could. I often sat with her, stroking her nose, watching her antics, or simply enjoying the silence. She "helped" put up festive decorations. We even participated in a local shelter's animal-art project.

Not long after that, I adopted Bella, a gray chinchilla rabbit whom I had fostered years earlier. Knowing her personality, I was sure that she and Ramona would get along well—and they did, becoming nearly inseparable.

Ramona was so lively with her new companion that it came as a real shock when Dr. Peg found a new lump the next summer. It was time to make a decision about further surgeries. Even though Ramona had recovered from the previous operations in a very timely manner, the surgeries were traumatic. Since the cancer would most likely continue to metastasize, I knew it would be unfair to repeatedly subject her to such invasive procedures. Dr. Peg and I decided this would be the last lumpectomy.

With Bella offering comfort and support, Ramona bounced back, eating and drinking as normal within a couple of days. It certainly helped that she liked the medication; she would come running to me to take it! Her energy seemed boundless.

I look at her today, tears of sadness mingled with tears of happiness. I consider the time spent with Ramona as a gift to both of us. Yet I can't help but wonder, *For how much longer?*

I cannot know that answer—and it doesn't seem to matter to Ramona. She races around the room and then runs over to greet her best friend, Bella. As I watch my happy rabbits, I cannot help but marvel at the sheer grit and joy that have kept Ramona alive.

It is a privilege to have this little bunny share our home for whatever time she has left. Her zest for life is amazing and inspiring—to me and to everyone who knows her. She is strong and brave, teaching all of us how to live courageously. She is inquisitive, amusing, and definitely feisty. She is our Ramona.

ABOUT RABBITS: cancer

Two common reproductive cancers—uterine and mammary adenocarcinoma—occur in unspayed female rabbits.

Unaltered female rabbits are at risk for uterine cancer by the time they are two years old, and the probability increases as they age: it is estimated that 60% of unaltered females will have cancer by age four, 80% by age five. The cancer is invasive, spreading to surrounding tissues and through the circulatory system to other sites, including the brain and bones.

Spaying reduces the risk of both uterine and mammary adenocarcinoma, a multi-centric cancer that spreads through the lymphatic system. A female rabbit has eight to twelve mammary glands and is less likely to experience this type of cancer if the spay occurs before age one.

An unaltered male rabbit may develop testicular cancer, so neutering at the appropriate age by a qualified vet is recommended. Both male and female rabbits can get many other types of cancer (e.g., lymphoma, fibrosarcoma, osteosarcoma) and any organ can be a primary site—or a secondary site as a result of metastasis. Cancer becomes a greater concern as a rabbit ages, though it can occur in young bunnies as well.

Drowned Rats

by Nancy LaRoche

I had just sat down to what was supposed to be my first leisurely breakfast that week when the phone rang. Envisioning my meal growing cold while someone chattered at me, I reluctantly answered.

To my surprise, the caller was Georgia, who along with her partner Steve operated Willow Run, one of the feed stores in our Colorado community. Her voice, usually low and calm, was uncharacteristically high-pitched.

". . . left them in a box, and I don't know what to do," she cried into the phone. "They're wet and cold, and I think some are dead. Can you come?"

I'd missed the beginning of the first sentence, but the panic in her voice sent me into high gear. "Coming!" I cried and dropped the handset into its cradle. Grabbing the keys, I ran to my car.

I was surprised by a cold, early spring sleet that had begun during the night. It quickly wet my shirt and pricked my arms with icy needles. But remembering the urgency in Georgia's voice, I didn't return for a jacket.

Five minutes later, I was shivering in the big, barn-like building that housed Willow Run's packaged goods. Georgia, a square-built woman, was kneeling over a wet cardboard box on the floor, dabbing a towel at some small dark lumps inside it. Instead of the tough-as-nails businesswoman that most people knew, she was now an "anxious mother," her usual response to an animal in distress.

This morning, fury animated her wide face. Looking up at me, she choked out, "Someone left them in this box outside the door. When the sleet began, it soaked them. I think they're hypothermic." Her voice shook with anger. Then, with fear creeping into her tone, she stated simply, "I don't know what to do."

The five cold, wet lumps that lay there were hardly bigger than the one in my throat and, like it, seemed frozen in place. Two of them kicked spasmodically, indicating the possibility of life, but in a manner that more strongly suggested the throes of death. *Drowned rats* was the phrase that popped into my head, but they were neither drowned (I hoped) nor rats. The tiny elongated ears that lay plastered to their shoulders indicated clearly that the icy blobs were baby bunnies.

For a moment, I was overwhelmed with horror and despair. *How could people abandon baby bunnies like this? Had they bought two rabbits and been assured that both were females, only to discover otherwise when a litter arrived? Or had they bought a single rabbit, not knowing she was already pregnant? Or maybe they had wanted their children to see the "miracle of birth," but had not wanted to take responsibility for the results of that birth.*

Since beginning my rabbit-rescue work, I had discovered that many unwanted rabbits come into the world in these ways, only to be abandoned. But I couldn't fathom how anyone could dump so much responsibility on someone else's doorstep or fail to care enough to assure the survival of the bunnies until someone found them.

Staring at the disaster before me, I felt hopelessly inadequate. I had so little experience. Most of what I knew about rabbits came from books. I had worked with rabbits at the Humane Society of Boulder Valley, but none of my limited skills prepared me for a situation like this. The subconscious, though, is a mysterious thing. It sometimes whispers to our conscious mind what we need to know in a given situation. Such was the case this day.

"Georgia, is the grooming room open?" I asked.

Without answering, Georgia grabbed a key from under the counter and unlocked the door to that room. I began running warm water into the sink. Hands shaking with fear and hope, I quickly immersed one of the blobs of wet fur and cold flesh, keeping the head above water, and gently massaged the small, plump body. The sudden, purposeful wiggling I felt as the tiny bit of bunny warmed was like a miracle. Georgia had already turned on the drying cage. I toweled the bunny and transferred him, or perhaps her, into it.

Three more times, I immersed and tenderly kneaded the small bodies. Georgia toweled them. Incredibly, four miniature white-and-gray fluff balls were now happily preening themselves in the warmth of the dryer, as if they had just wakened from a nap and needed to put a few hairs back in place. Short forelegs stretched to clean adorable little faces, able to reach only the chins and whiskers. Tiny feet pulled delicate, upright ears down to be carefully cleaned by pink tongues. Bright, alert eyes gazed at us all the while. Their expressions looking at us were very much like ours looking at them—expressions that might be interpreted as, "How fascinating you are!"

Twisting to one side and then the other, the baby rabbits shifted their efforts from faces to backs and sides. Then they stretched improbably long hind legs forward, spreading their toes while busily grooming each one. When finished, the bunnies seemed to pause for a moment, as if contemplating what to do next.

Suddenly, one bunny shot unexpectedly into the air, as if a spring had been released beneath him. Then another popped. Soon all four were leaping and falling over each other, expressing the joy of life in which rabbits seem to specialize.

Sadly, the fifth bunny was another story. I had immersed him and massaged, but there had been no answering wiggles, only a tiny spasm and then a small limp body, lifeless on a towel. Tears blinded me as I dried him, inwardly cursing my helplessness to do anything more than to restore a bit of fluffiness to his reddish-brown coat.

Four were alive and apparently well, but I keenly felt the loss of this fifth one. Had the five been stuffed toy animals, losing one wouldn't have mattered so much. But this had been a sentient being, endowed with the same desire to live and the same abilities to think and feel that are shared by all animals. He was important as an individual and the survival of his siblings did not lessen the loss of *him.*

Fluffing his coat, I wondered about my need to do so. *Was I trying to disguise death? Was it an apology for my inability to catch that last spark of life and fan it into a flame?* Perhaps it was nothing more than an expression of sorrow.

"I'm so sorry, little one," I whispered. "So very, very sorry."

As I turned back, seeking comfort in the sight of the cute, living bunnies, Steve came in to check on how things were going. He had seen the box with its miserable contents and was anxious to know whether our efforts had been

successful. Observing the four, he said, "Well, four out of five isn't bad." And then he looked at the little body on the counter where I had left it and added, "But five out of five is great!"

For an instant, the significance of his last words failed to register. Then my gaze whipped to the little body on the counter—there, before my amazed eyes, the tiny creature was struggling to his feet. A surge of gratitude for a life returned swept over me. Breathless with wonder, I put him with his siblings, where he joined them in their grooming rituals.

When the bunnies were fully dry, Georgia turned off the drying cage and fetched a dish of pellets, alfalfa hay, and a low crock of water, placing all on the floor within easy reach of the bunnies. They nibbled hungrily while we watched in rapt delight. Tummies full, they tumbled together, each struggling to bury him- or herself beneath the others. A few moments later, there was only a soft pile of fur, with a couple of unexpected ears and legs sticking out at random angles, motionless except for a gentle rise and fall indicating sound sleep.

My elation was inexpressible. Georgia's and Steve's beaming faces and the sight of five healthy bunnies made me feel like some sort of miracle worker. Few things I had done in my life seemed as meaningful as helping these furry little babies return to playing, eating, and sleeping, as if it were just another day in their young lives.

Which, thankfully, it was.

ABOUT RABBITS: keeping a bunny clean

Although a warm water bath was used as an emergency measure in this story, as a general rule a rabbit should not be immersed in water. The experience is so stressful that a bunny is likely to become ill. In addition, a rabbit who gets wet to the skin becomes easily chilled and can go into shock, which can be lethal. The only way to ensure a rabbit is completely dry is to use a professional drying cage (as was done for the baby bunnies in this story).

If a bunny cannot groom herself, the caregiver can help by lifting the fur with one hand, then gently combing the fine hairs out from under that hand with a comb. In the event that a rabbit is soiled with feces, some fur may need to be cut off—but extreme care must be taken so that the rabbit's skin is not lifted into the path of the scissors or electric shears. If a rabbit is soiled with urine, it may be necessary to spot wash the area, using a towel to blot water from the fur and maintaining the rabbit in a warm space until she is completely dry. Stained fur will likely remain until the rabbit molts and grows new fur.

AFTERWORD

So You're Thinking about Getting a Rabbit. . .

Rabbits are full of personality and *joie de vivre*! After reading about how much fun they are, you may think that living with a house rabbit is something you would like to try.

STOP! Don't act on impulse. Though living with companion rabbits can be a terrific experience, they require a big investment in time, attention, and special care. Because of their physical construction and prey mentality, rabbits are very different from the cats and dogs with whom so many of us share our lives.

Before bringing a bunny home, do some serious research. Think it over and be honest with yourself: can you commit to meeting all of a rabbit's needs, including expense, for the duration of his or her lifespan? Can you provide a safe and loving home as well as time for interactive socializing? Rabbits are wonderful animals, but they do not fit every lifestyle.

Love Your Rabbit

The Basics of Rabbit Care

Human guardian

The rabbit's safety and care should be managed by a responsible adult. An attentive caregiver understands and appreciates the independent nature and prey responses of rabbits.

Companionship

Rabbits are very social creatures; they need friends and playtime. They are most active at dawn and dusk and generally take a midday nap, making it natural to engage with them before and after work or school.

Socialization

In addition to establishing a good relationship with a rabbit for the fun of interacting with him, it is critical that the human caretaker be able to pick up the bunny for grooming and in the event of a health problem. A rabbit must be handled gently and correctly to prevent injury.

Veterinarian

A vet who is knowledgeable about rabbits is essential, and back-up emergency care is just as important.

Spay/neuter

"Altering" a rabbit reduces health risks, results in fewer behavior problems, and stops the cycle of overpopulation. Because some rabbits can reach sexual maturity by 2-1/2 months, males and females should be kept separated from the age of 10 weeks until they can be neutered by a vet experienced in treating rabbits.

Proper diet and fresh water	Each rabbit's diet should be based on age, weight, activity level, and predisposition to health problems. Rabbits are herbivores, with the appropriate diet consisting of grass hay, limited pellets, green leafy vegetables, and fresh water. They should be allowed to eat the nutrient-rich cecotropes from their anus, as the cecotropes are *not* fecal waste.
Bunny-proofing	This is essential for the safety of the rabbit and to prevent damage to your home. Never assume a rabbit's lack of interest in an item means she will always avoid that object.
Items for chewing and digging	Observe what attracts your rabbit's attention. In addition to grass hay, provide additional chewing items such as untreated grass mats and willow baskets. Make a digging box: a covered box with a hole cut into the side, filled with paper litter.
Play spaces	Be creative! Rabbits love tubes, low ramps, baskets, and boxes with holes cut into them. Change the configuration to pique interest. Give them running space.
Housing	A rabbit's home should be large enough so he can stretch out, stand up, and move about; there also needs to be room for an appropriately sized litter box. Rabbits also benefit from solid flooring, not wire.
Location of home	The condo should be located away from drafts, direct heat, full sun, and high-pitched and/or loud noises, but (ideally) situated so that the rabbit can observe and participate in family interactions.
Cleanliness of home	Clean the condo when the rabbits are outside of it. A dilute solution of vinegar and water is safe; rinse well, then dry.
Litter box	The box should be sized to the rabbit. Paper litters or wood stove pellets are appropriate litters. Avoid clay and aromatic litters (e.g., cedar shavings) and materials that rabbits will eat (e.g., wheat and corn litters).

Rabbits + Classrooms = Mismatch

The following article was written because of Kali, the rabbit who inspired this book. She was born in a preschool classroom, removed too young from her mother, put alone into a cage in another classroom, and then not given proper care. It is my hope that this article will help prevent such misfortune from befalling another hapless bunny.

"Mismatch" means to *match unsuitably or inaccurately*, and most classrooms (including preschool rooms) happen to be very unsuitable "homes" for rabbits. *Why?* A few facts may help explain.

- Rabbits are prey animals, and most humans are unfamiliar with prey psychology. Projecting expectations of predator (dog and cat) behaviors onto rabbits creates misconceptions and misunderstandings about bunnies' natural temperament and behaviors.

- Rabbits are culturally viewed as sweet, cuddly, and gentle. Although this is certainly part of their nature, in other respects they are quite the opposite: independent and strong-willed, feisty and territorial, and sometimes aggressive or grouchy (especially if not neutered or spayed).

- Although domestic bunnies cannot survive in the wild, they retain many of the instincts inherited from their European wild rabbit ancestors. For example, they instinctively nap during the day, and they innately dig and chew.

- Rabbits' chewing behavior, which some people view solely as destructive, is spurred by physiology. Their teeth, which grow continuously throughout life, are made for chewing fibrous, coarse, and abrasive plant materials, such as grass hay. The action of the teeth grinding together as tough plant materials are consumed helps maintain the proper length and shape of the teeth. Both proper diet and veterinary care are critical for preventing the health issues that can result from tooth overgrowth.

Here are some of the ways in which the needs of rabbits and the needs of children diverge, creating a mismatch.

- Rabbits are crepuscular, a zoological reference to being naturally active before sunrise and at twilight.
  Children (and most teachers) are generally out of the classroom during those times, depriving the resident bunny of the opportunities to interact socially and to exercise outside the cage during his normal active time.

- Rabbits need a safe, open exercise space.
  Most classrooms are not bunny-proofed, which can result in damage to the room—and injury or death to the rabbit. Depending on the classroom configuration, desks, cabinets, and other furniture may allow only minimal exercise space and may pose potential safety concerns for a free-roaming rabbit. In addition, the bunny can be accidentally sat on, kicked, or stepped on as adults and children participate in classroom activities.

- Rabbits, as prey animals, instinctively seek their safe place and are often territorial about their home.
  Children want to show their love and attention by trying to pet the bunny and often stick their finger, pencil, or other object through the wire sides of the cage. Such actions are very stressful and unsafe for a rabbit—and unsafe for the children, as the rabbit may lunge and bite as a means of defense.

- Rabbits need a regular routine and predictable surroundings.
  Children proudly take the bunny home for a weekend, not realizing how frightening the strange noises, odors, other household animals, and unfamiliar routines are to a rabbit. Separating two rabbits who live together in the classroom and sending each one home to a different family creates incredible stress for the bunnies. However, leaving a rabbit alone in the classroom for a weekend or holiday puts the rabbit in jeopardy, since these delicate creatures need daily care and monitoring.

- Rabbits instinctively hide signs of illness or injury.

  It's easy for a busy teacher or classroom aide to miss the subtle, but critical, signs of a sick or hurt rabbit. Sending a bunny home with students for weekends, holidays, or vacation can result in the signs of illness or injury being overlooked or ignored. If there are other animals in the home, the rabbit may be exposed to trans-species ailments.

- Rabbits are considered "exotics" in veterinary terminology, and they need regular check-ups by vets who know rabbits well.

  It is incumbent upon the teacher to obtain proper medical care for a classroom rabbit. School district funds are not generally allocated for animal care, which places the financial burden on the teacher. If the rabbit's health needs are not met, children may inadvertently learn that it is okay to have animals even if one cannot properly care for them.

- Rabbits have fragile bodies and must be handled carefully to prevent injury.

  Youngsters are very eager, do not know their own strength, and often do not respect a rabbit's needs. A child tends to grab and hold a bunny improperly and too tightly.

- Rabbits have delicate, complex digestive systems and may become ill, and even die, from eating the wrong foods.

  Children are frequently allowed to give foods that the teacher may not realize are inappropriate. In an attempt to be "friends," a child might sneak forbidden/toxic foods or too many treats to the rabbit.

- Rabbits require a quality high-fiber diet, and grass hay should be available at all times. Pellets and fresh leafy green vegetables are also part of the diet, based on the bunny's age, weight, and health.

  Hay creates a mess, poses storage problems, and may trigger allergies in some children and adults. Leafy greens require refrigeration.

- Though healthy rabbits groom themselves, some assistance is needed, especially when the bunny is molting. Long-haired breeds require special attention.

  Grooming should be performed on a routine basis. Proper grooming of a long-haired rabbit is time-consuming and should occur daily when the rabbit is shedding and at least weekly during the rest of the year. Children and adults may have allergic reactions to rabbit fur.

- Rabbits are intelligent, inquisitive, social beings who need stimulation, freedom, and lots of interaction. Most teachers' main focus is, understandably, on the students—not on keeping a classroom rabbit challenged and stimulated. No one may notice that the isolated bunny is lonely and depressed.

Before bringing a rabbit into the classroom, a teacher should honestly ask him- or herself: Why do I want a bunny in the classroom? What exactly am I using him to teach?

It may be that the teacher wishes to model responsible behavior or to provide an experience for children who, for various reasons, don't have a companion animal at home. Or perhaps the instructor wants students to research rabbits, and then apply that learning to other topics. Sometimes the true answer may be that the rabbit is not really for teaching purposes, but rather for entertainment or novelty in the classroom.

In all cases, there is a need for a sincere answer to additional questions: Can I ensure that *all* the needs of the rabbit—a high maintenance companion animal—will be properly met? Do I want a rabbit as part of my family, and am I willing to take the bunny home with me each day? Many times, the answer will be "no" and alternative teaching solutions should be found.

Animal rescue organizations receive calls both during and after the school year regarding classroom rabbits needing a home. Or, as happens too often, the teacher may "award" the classroom bunny to a student whose family may know nothing about the care or needs of a rabbit. If the situation does not work out, the well-meaning family may hope the bunny finds a new home through the local animal shelter or may even harbor the common misconception that domestic rabbits can survive in the wild.

Therefore, a teacher should also address the following: If the rabbit has to be relinquished for *any* reason, what will happen to him? For example, what will happen to the bunny at the end of the semester or school year or if I should happen to leave my teaching position? What if someone in the classroom is allergic to the rabbit's fur or to the hay? What will I do if a student is not gentle enough to be safely near the bunny or if the frightened rabbit bites a child? Am I personally willing to give the bunny a permanent, loving home to ensure he does not end up an unwanted rabbit, consigned to a hutch, taken to a shelter (where he may be euthanized), or abandoned outdoors (where he will die unless rescued)?

It is also important to consider the students and their feelings. How will they react if the rabbit has to be removed from the classroom for any reason or if the rabbit becomes ill and dies? Addressing such potentially traumatic situations with students requires time, patience, understanding, and love.

Rabbits and classrooms are generally a serious mismatch because the nature and requirements of a rabbit and the realities and needs of students are fundamentally incompatible—unless the teacher is unusually committed to making the experience as good for the rabbit as for the students. In contrast, a rabbit will thrive in a home that honors the needs for affection, health, safety, and free expression of the bunny's multifaceted nature.

Velly Oliver

Modeling Love and Respect for a Classroom Rabbit

by Cheryl Rosemary Abbott

When I wrote my article about rabbits in the classroom ("Rabbits + Classrooms = Mismatch*"), I had not met Cheryl Abbott, a teacher in the Atlanta area. I contacted her after reading an article in the North Georgia House Rabbit Society's newsletter about how she guides her students in respecting the animals who share their school room. I am pleased that she offered to write the following article, for the benefit of teachers and parents alike.*

From personal experience, I know that having a rabbit in the classroom can be a wonderful learning opportunity for the children, even though providing proper care for the rabbit requires a tremendous amount of time and energy from the teacher. With most of us being incredibly busy people—managing curriculum, providing discipline, and tackling (seeming) mountains of paperwork in addition to other tasks—we must still consider seriously our responsibility to the bunny, including financial aspects of care. All animals require veterinary care, and a rabbit with health problems can become very expensive.

I know many horror stories about teachers who did not take care of their classroom pets: forgetting to give them water, leaving electrical cords exposed, or not supervising proper handling by the children. I am afraid many teachers think, "Oh that's someone else's class, not mine." But, sadly, an injured or dead animal is a very likely scenario in many classrooms. I believe that to have a healthy, happy rabbit, teachers must be totally committed to caring for the animal in every way. I discourage anyone from taking on the added responsibility of having an animal in the classroom unless he or she is willing to do whatever it takes to ensure the creature's wellbeing.

I got my first rabbit by default when the owner of the private school where I was teaching came in with a cute brown lop-eared rabbit named Maverick. I was shocked to see that he was kept in a two- by three-foot wire cage and that the children interacted with him by poking sticks into the cage and yelling. Whenever I released him, Maverick followed me all around the room. Although he was friendly and dear, I knew he would not thrive if he remained in that situation. Luckily, the school's owner was willing to part with him, and I took my new companion home to my family.

Cheryl Rosemary Abbott

Cleo in her "safe area." She has a place to retreat and nap, but Cleo can come out whenever she wants.

The next year I taught a kindergarten class in an inner city school, and I brought Maverick with me once or twice a week. Many of the kids were afraid of him because they had never been around animals. In that classroom, I had five abused and neglected kids to whom the bunny brought joy and love beyond words. I did not allow Maverick to run around the classroom; instead, I had the students go into his fenced area one at a time to pet him.

With such a presence of love in the room, I saw a complete change in the nature of the classroom. I watched and listened as the toughest child melted while gently petting this small animal and as the children shared their problems with Maverick (big ears hear everything). I also found that our bunny was a source of consolation when they were hurt. I enjoyed seeing them discover that their rabbit was a comfort and a companion. Whenever I ask my students what they like best about school, I always hear the name of our rabbit.

As I have already mentioned, the benefits of having a classroom pet must always be balanced by the teacher's unwavering commitment, care, and genuine concern for the rabbit's needs. With our students looking to us as role models, we must show them how to love and respect other beings. One important way to do this is to treat the rabbit as a treasured family member and take him or her home from the classroom every night.

A RABBIT FOR THE CLASSROOM

Finding a rabbit who has the right temperament for a classroom is not easy. It is important to spend time with the bunny to see whether there is a good fit with your class and whether car travel to and from the school causes too much stress for your pet. Your rabbit also needs you to spend time at home building a firm, trusting relationship, as well as teaching him or her to come when called and to use the litter pan. The bunny should be spayed or neutered, and a vet examination will check for parasites, ear mites, structural problems, and other issues.

TWO IMPORTANT COMMAND WORDS

One useful command word is "Home," which I use when I want the rabbit to go back inside her fenced area. It is not safe for a rabbit to be running around the classroom if the teacher cannot be consistently attentive to the bunny's actions. People may come in and leave the door open. The rabbit might get into something she shouldn't. My current classroom rabbit, Cleo, always goes back in her safe area when the children go out for recess, for lunch, or if the students are doing something active (like dancing).

To train Cleo, I have designated one place in the room as her home, and I reinforce it by tapping and saying "Home" whenever she is in that area. With enough repetition—and initially with a treat such as a bit of parsley or kale—she has learned to go home on command. Now that she understands, the treat is not needed as Cleo just goes home when told to do so. She also goes home naturally when she is scared or wants to get away from the kids and be by herself. I think that to her, "Home" is her safe haven.

The second command word, "Up," is used because rabbits are natural ground-dwellers and are usually frightened when lifted off the ground. Generally, when you want to cuddle your rabbit, do it on the floor. Later, when a degree of trust is established, the rabbit may want to be cuddled on your lap in a chair—but not always. Some rabbits always prefer the floor and this should be respected. In a classroom with younger or less mature children, handling the rabbit while seated on the floor is the safest bet.

Whenever I pick up Cleo, the process starts with putting a hand on each side of her body, saying "Up," and giving her about ten seconds to prepare herself to be picked up (bottom and chest supported). Having this time to prepare makes a huge difference for the rabbit. Consistently using this method reassures the rabbit that there is no chance of being picked up if you have not said the word "up." She can trust that you will not do *that thing* unless she hears the word first.

GETTING THE CLASSROOM READY

A rabbit cannot stay in a cage and be healthy; a bunny must have exercise. This poses special challenges for the classroom. *Before* a rabbit comes to school, the entire room needs to be made safe (bunny-proofed) by removing, blocking, or covering anything potentially harmful. Rabbits instinctively need to chew, and a live wire can cause electrical shock or death. Electrical cords should be covered; PVC elbows can cover the plugs, while straight PVC pipe protects cords as far up as the bunny can reach. Flexible plastic electrical conduit can also be used. The hardest cords to cover are those to the computers. By using duct tape, all the cords can be adhered to the top of the computer tables so the hard plastic cover is needed only from the electrical outlet to the table itself. If there are cords that cannot be covered, a barrier can be put up to prevent the rabbit from accessing them.

Rabbits often like to chew books. Therefore, valued books should be shelved higher than the rabbit's reach. In my room, there are lots of paperback books for the kids to read, and a nibble here or there does not make much difference. Books from the media center, however, require higher shelves for protection.

For Cleo's first few days in class, she stayed in her safe area. This part of the classroom is fenced and includes a litter box, food and water, rattan rugs (safe to chew), toys, and a place to hide. Rabbits should be provided a place to retreat, one that cannot be reached by the children. Cleo has a little house where she cannot be disturbed, so she can be with the kids some of the time but can also nap whenever she wants.

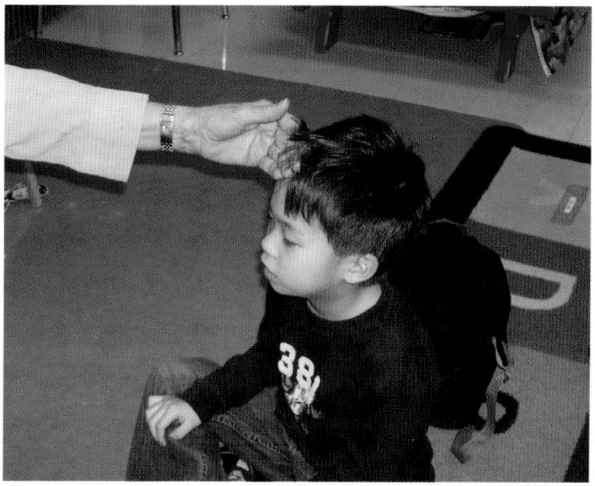

Cheryl Rosemary Abbott

I am demonstrating to Charles the gentle pressure to use when petting Cleo.

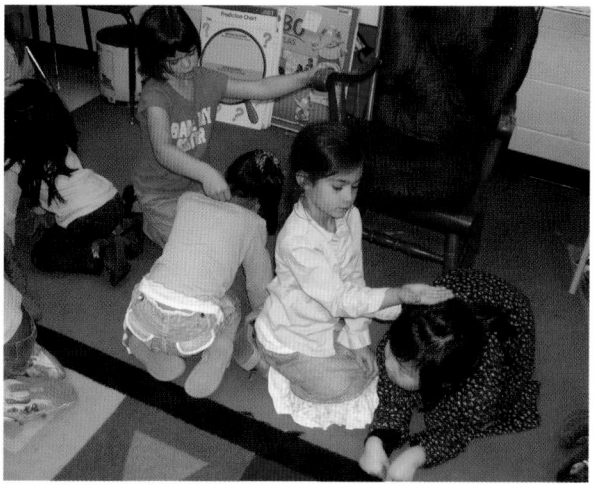

Cheryl Rosemary Abbott

A group of kids practicing on each other.

Cheryl Rosemary Abbott

The students are learning to gently pet Cleo on the floor.

In Cleo's safe area, there are both a bowl for her to drink from and a back-up water bottle. Why two water sources? When rabbits do not have enough water, they can quickly become dehydrated. If the water level gets too low in one container, having a back-up water source can help prevent tragedy. The importance of having clean water available at all times cannot be stressed enough.

Since I have a large classroom and I want the rabbit to be able to quickly reach a litter pan, there is an extra one under a computer table. The table provides some protection and an out-of-the-way feel. But the main purpose of having an extra litter box—located on the opposite side of the room from the rabbit's safe area—is to prevent fecal pellets on the classroom floor. Speaking of which, when a rabbit does "make a mistake," the kids are taught to get a tissue, pick up the dry, nearly odorless fecal pellet, and throw it in the trash. If the children know the procedure, they do not create a fuss when it happens. For the most part, having two litter pans in the room is all that is needed. I change Cleo's litter pans each day after the kids leave school.

GETTING THE KIDS READY

One of the most common mistakes teachers make is not training students how to interact with a bunny *before* he or she comes to school. Children must be taught to be sensitive to a rabbit's needs, especially the fact that the animal can be easily frightened. Teaching children to talk quietly, move slowly, stroke gently, and be respectful are life skills that reach far beyond the classroom.

Students follow the teacher's lead. Be sure to model the behavior you expect from them. In preparation for the introduction of the rabbit, I demonstrate how to caress the bunny by using the *back* of my hand and stroking the children from between their eyes to the top of their forehead. They love the feel of the gentle stroke and understand why a rabbit likes it. When I see the kids petting Cleo gently, I know the lesson was a success.

Before Cleo first came to class, there were many discussions with the children about how they needed to act around her. Here are the rules my kindergarten students agreed on:

1. Talk softly
2. Pet gently on top of Cleo's head or back
3. No picking her up
4. No poking
5. No running toward Cleo or her home
6. Crawl around on the floor whenever Cleo is out of her home (her safe area).

After her first week in the fenced area, Cleo was given the run of the classroom, and the children had to follow rule #6. Young children run without even realizing it and can fall for no apparent reason, either of which can spell disaster for the bunny. The kids love following rule #6, crawling from table to table if it means that they may encounter a bunny. Cleo runs over to children while they are crawling, and they love both having a bunny to snuggle with while reading on the floor and delivering an extra pet before moving to the next group.

When I taught second grade, the rules were different. The tables were closer together and the children sat for longer periods of time. In a classroom with older students, the rabbit can be allowed free run of the room as long as the children are sitting quietly at their desks and can generally watch out for the bunny. Of course it still depends on the class. Some classes would require the same strict rules that apply to a kindergarten classroom. Even if the class is generally calm, when the students are doing anything active or if I am not in the room, the bunny is placed back into her safe area.

My class clearly understands that the rabbit never goes home or stays overnight with a student; Cleo *always* goes home with me. Years ago, I had a wonderful classroom hamster named Mozart. He went home for spring break with a family I highly trusted, got out of his cage, became lost in the house, and died. Needless to say, the family was devastated. The children in my classroom blamed the child for "killing Mozart," and trying to convince them otherwise was a nightmare. That was the first and last time one of my classroom animals went home with anyone else. Not only can accidents happen but, even more basically, rabbits need familiarity and routine. Going home with others can trigger enough stress to cause illness in a bunny. In addition, even the most well-meaning animal lover may not know the special needs of rabbits. The potential for trauma, illness, or death is not worth the novelty of a home visit.

THE CARE OF A CLASSROOM RABBIT

My classroom has a rotating helper chart. One of the items on the chart is "Cleo's helper." This is a highly coveted job. The child who is Cleo's helper goes into the rabbit's safe area and changes the water bowl and bottle, puts the allotted food into Cleo's dish, fills her hay bin, straightens her rugs, and picks up her toys. When the student is done, he or she can sit on the floor and pet the bunny. The children love doing this!

After the child finishes the assigned tasks, it is important for me to make sure that everything has been done correctly—because, ultimately, the teacher is responsible for the rabbit. This really is the bottom line. Someone has to be the main caregiver and that person is the classroom teacher. Kids are kids, and it is not reasonable to expect them to care for a rabbit the way an adult would. While it is true that the older the child, the greater the possibility that everything will be done right, it is still the teacher's responsibility to check. Furthermore, rabbits hide signs of illness and injury, and it is through daily interaction that I monitor Cleo's health.

Death by illness, injury, or age is an ever-present possibility for your classroom rabbit and can be a potentially difficult situation. Speaking about death with the children can be an educational experience; some parents have written letters thanking me for helping their child express grief. However, depending on your approach and on the demographics of your community, it may become an issue of contention.

Cheryl Rosemary Abbott

Catherine crawling over to pet Cleo.

After a classroom animal dies, I notify the parents in the event they want to discuss the death with their child. To assist the children in processing their feelings about the death, they write letters and draw pictures to say good-bye. Our beloved pet is then buried in a hole dug by the custodian in the woods behind the school playground. When my last classroom rabbit passed away due to old age, she was put in a box with some of her toys. The children held hands in a circle and talked about their experiences with her. They put their letters on top of the box, and we cried. It was both a cathartic and a bonding process.

On the whole, having a rabbit in the classroom can be a fantastic experience for the children. Your goal as the responsible adult is to ensure that it is a wonderful treat for the rabbit as well. Do not take this mission lightly. The responsibility is great, but the rewards are even greater.

Veterinary Care: Rabbit Basics

Note that this article contains only very basic information and that some of it may change as new protocols are developed; an experienced rabbit vet can provide guidance.

Companion rabbits now live longer, healthier lives thanks to both medical advances and a better understanding of rabbits' nature and needs. The general lifespan of a rabbit who receives good care is eight to twelve years (with some living longer), though individual characteristics, genetics, and standard of care may shorten some rabbits' lives.

Rabbits hide signs of illness so look for early warning signs such as decreased intake of food, lesser amounts of or smaller-than-normal-size fecal pellets, and loud gurgling sounds from the stomach area. More subtle clinical signs include breathing difficulty or shallow, rapid breathing and uncharacteristically remaining in one place. Knowing what is normal behavior for your rabbit will assist you in detecting problems that may arise.

Qualified veterinary care is incredibly important; do your homework and interview potential vets. Find out for how many years the person has been treating rabbits, how often a specific condition has been treated or a particular procedure has been performed, and whether he or she is willing to consult with another veterinarian if necessary. In addition to your regular vet, locate another experienced veterinarian as backup in the event your regular vet is unavailable.

SOME GENERAL INFORMATION

- Most veterinarians discuss a rabbit's diet with their clients because the appropriate diet can prevent numerous health problems.

- Rabbits do not tolerate pain well and, for many conditions, an analgesic (pain medication) will allow them to recover faster and resume eating sooner.

- Spaying or neutering is recommended for all companion rabbits in good health.

- Check-ups generally include the rabbit's weight; dental, eye, and ear exam; lung and heart evaluation; abdominal palpation; and a body exam for lumps or other abnormalities. Baseline bloodwork (i.e., CBC, chemistry, bacterial/parasite disease screening) and a stool check are sometimes recommended.

TESTS, DIAGNOSIS, AND SEDATION

- Bloodwork can help diagnose problems such as liver or kidney disease, infection or inflammation, anemia, and electrolyte imbalance.

- Radiographs (x-rays) can help diagnose heart problems, pneumonia, arthritis, fracture or dislocation, intestinal stasis or obstruction, foreign body, dental disease, ovarian disease or cancer, kidney or bladder/urinary tract stones, and urinary sludge.

- Ultrasound looks at the internal structure of soft tissue organs (e.g., liver, spleen, adrenal glands, kidneys, and bladder) for abnormalities such as tumors, abscesses, and stones. Ultrasound can also assess some organs (e.g., heart function or peristaltic waves in the gut).

- Rabbits are anesthetized for a thorough molar examination and surgeries such as spay and neuter; they are sometimes sedated or anesthetized for radiographs (x-rays) and collection of laboratory samples.

MEDICATIONS, INCLUDING FOR PAIN

The *Exotic Animal Formulary* and medical textbooks provide guidelines on medications for rabbits. When questions arise, consulting with another vet or a good veterinary teaching hospital will help.

It is important to monitor for any signs of drug intolerance; a common sign is cecotropes that are unusually soft. Discuss any such changes with your vet.

- These medications are *unsafe* for rabbits: cephalosporins (e.g., cephalexin, Cefa-Drops®), clindamycin, erythromycin, lincomycin, and tilmicosin.

- Rabbits should *never* be given any form of oral penicillin. The only penicillin that is safe is the injectable form, which is commonly used to treat abscesses.

- With long-term use of an antibiotic, a probiotic is sometimes prescribed for its gastrointestinal (GI) benefits.

Pain causes stress in a rabbit, reducing appetite and decreasing gut motility. These, in turn, can lead to serious or fatal conditions. Some rabbits show pain by grinding their teeth and/or adopting a hunched position; others hide or sit quietly, as if resting.

The two main groups of analgesics are opioids and non-steroidal anti-inflammatory drugs (NSAIDs). The prescribed pain medication will be specific to the particular medical treatment as well as to the health of the rabbit. In some cases, both an opioid and a NSAID will be used.

SURGICAL ISSUES

Having a quiet space for rabbits at the animal hospital will help reduce their stress. Having a bunny buddy usually helps comfort a rabbit and, in some cases, may be key in the rabbit's survival.

Rabbits are seldom kept overnight at an animal hospital because vets know that recovery generally happens more rapidly in the familiarity of home. If a rabbit must remain at the hospital, recovery in a quiet area—away from the sounds and smells of predators—will help reduce stress.

- Rabbits should *not* be fasted; they should be allowed to eat and drink prior to surgery. The exception would be for abdominal surgery, when food may be withheld for 1-2 hours pre-operatively. Food residue should be removed from the mouth prior to surgery.

- After surgery, eating and drinking should be encouraged. If the rabbit is in pain, syringe-feeding may be necessary.

- Pain medication is pivotal to a rabbit's recovery and return to a normal eating and drinking routine.

- During and immediately after surgery, a rabbit's temperature is likely to drop, and supplemental heat is essential to keep the body temperature stable.

LEARN FROM YOUR VET

In cases where rabbits require repeated injections and fluids, caregivers can often learn how to administer these at home, thus reducing the bunny's stress due to frequent trips to the animal hospital. It is also a good idea to become knowledgeable about syringe feeding and to keep a nutritive formula on hand for that purpose.

If you have a stethoscope, have your vet demonstrate proper use as well as the difference between normal and abnormal gut sounds. It is extremely difficult to determine lung sounds, and x-rays may be required for assessment. Similarly, evaluating a rabbit's heart is very difficult due to the rapid rate; other diagnostics will be required if a heart condition is suspected. When there are signs of a clinical problem, take your bunny to the vet as soon as possible.

This article was written with the assistance of Drs. Wendy Asato, Thomas Chlebecek, Hillary Cook, Bill Guerrera, and Angela Lennox.

Rabbit Teeth: The Importance of Proper Care

by Angela M. Lennox, DVM Dipl. ABVP-Avian
Past president of the Association of Exotic Mammal Veterinarians

Rabbits' teeth affect a wide variety of health issues. Some of the stories in this book include rabbits who suffered such cruel neglect that their deaths were imminent. In two such accounts, people skilled in caring for rabbits provided emergency measures, including clipping the incisors. Under normal circumstances, this type of home dental care is strongly discouraged, as it carries a high risk of tooth fracture and abscess.

The most unique feature of rabbit teeth is that both the incisors (front teeth) and the molars (cheek teeth) grow continually throughout the life of the rabbit. Maintaining the normal length and shape of these ever-growing teeth is accomplished in healthy rabbits as the teeth grind against each other, especially when crushing very fibrous plant materials like grass hay. Although the causes of molar overgrowth and uneven growth are not definitive, lack of fiber (hay) in the diet is almost certainly a factor.

When molars wear unevenly and overgrow, chewing puts excessive pressure on the roots. The resulting damage can predispose the tooth to fracture and abscess. Diseased teeth often bend and grow in abnormal directions, which can result in damage to soft tissues, including the tongue and cheeks. All these dental disorders cause significant pain, weight loss, and debilitation.

Overgrowth of the incisors can be caused by congenital malformation of the jaw (especially in rabbits bred for shortened facial structure, such as lop and dwarf breeds) or by overgrowth of the cheek teeth. Elongated incisors generally grow in abnormal directions, causing soft tissue injury, pain, and impaired ability to eat.

In cases of congenital jaw malformation, extraction of the incisors is often the best treatment. Rabbits without incisors generally do very well, moving the food with their lips and tongue to the back of the mouth and then chewing it with their molars.

Dental disease is a serious health issue and must be treated by a veterinarian skilled in this area of rabbit medicine and surgery. The small size of a rabbit's mouth and the presence of cheek folds limit the examination of all the molars, and sedation is frequently necessary. Veterinarians experienced in treating rabbits use specialized equipment to examine teeth and treat disorders, including high-speed dental burrs to shorten and shape the teeth. In addition to carrying a high risk of tooth fracture and abscess, clipping overgrown teeth with nail clippers or rongeurs neither allows teeth to be restored to normal shape nor addresses underlying issues such as infection.

Rabbits are complex little beings, and their health issues are very different from those of cats and dogs. Therefore, finding a qualified vet to treat your rabbit is of paramount importance. The Association of Exotic Mammal Veterinarians (AEMV) has been working with the American Board of Veterinary Practitioners (ABVP) to establish an Exotic Companion Mammal Specialty. As of 2009, exotic practitioners who apply for and successfully pass the rigorous testing process will be able to distinguish themselves as "rabbit specialists." For additional information, go to www.abvp.com and www.aemv.org.

Special Thanks

AUTHORS

Michael W. Fox, DSc, PhD, BVetMed, MRCVS, contributed the Foreword to this book. An expert in both medicine and psychology, Dr. Fox's training includes a degree in veterinary medicine as well as doctorate degrees in medicine and animal behavior/ethology. A strong advocate of animal rights, bioethics, and environmental protection, Dr. Fox is a veterinary consultant to various environmental and animal-related organizations and lectures internationally on topics ranging from canine behavior and animal rights to sustainable agriculture and safe food. A frequent guest on national television and radio network shows, Dr. Fox is also the syndicated columnist of "Animal Doctor," published in newspapers across the US. A recipient of the Christopher Award for children's literature for *The Wolf*, Dr. Fox has authored more than 40 books. They encompass a wide scope of work, from the behavior of wild canids to understanding dogs and cats, and from animal care to bioethics. Some of his works are: *The Soul of the Wolf*; *The Healing Touch for Dogs*; *The Healing Touch for Cats*; *The Boundless Circle*; *Eating with Conscience*; *Dog Body, Dog Mind*; and *Cat Body, Cat Mind*. Dr. Fox coauthored *Not Fit for a Dog: The Truth About Manufactured Dog and Cat Food* with Elizabeth Hodgkins, DVM, and Marion E. Smart, DVM PhD.

Cheryl Rosemary Abbott (contributor of "Modeling Love and Respect for a Classroom Rabbit") is a National Board Certified Teacher with both master's and specialist degrees in early childhood education; she teaches elementary students in the Atlanta, Georgia, area. Cheryl is a volunteer with the North Georgia House Rabbit Society and has written articles for their newsletter.

Angela M. Lennox, DVM Dipl. ABVP-Avian, ("Rabbit Teeth: The Importance of Proper Care") has practiced avian and exotic animal medicine exclusively since 1991. As an adjunct professor at Purdue University School of Veterinary Medicine, she teaches a variety of topics in exotic animal medicine and surgery, as well as presenting at conferences and lecturing internationally. Dr. Lennox is coauthor of *Clinical Radiology of Exotic Companion Mammals* and editor of *Rabbit and Rodent Dentistry Handbook*. Her articles have been published in various journals, including *Veterinary Clinics of North America: Avian and Exotic Practice, Seminars in Exotic Pet Medicine, Journal of Exotic Pet Medicine*, and *Exotic DVM*. Dr. Lennox is past president of the Association of Exotic Mammal Veterinarians (www.aemv.org), an organization dedicated to improving the standards of exotic mammal medicine and surgery.

SUSAN CHERNAK MCELROY ("Emily") is a well-known speaker, facilitator, and best-selling author. Her books include *Animals as Teachers and Healers, Animals as Guides for the Soul, All My Relations*, and *Why Buffalo Dance*. Her writing is also featured in many of the *Chicken Soup* volumes and in several anthologies, including *Kinship with the Animals, Wounded Healers*, and *Intimate Nature: The Bond between Women and Animals*. Susan's life work is deeply influenced by her enchantment with and love of animals and nature, her personal experience with cancer, and her studies in indigenous traditions. For more information about Susan, please visit her website at www.susanchernakmcelroy.com.

BERNIE S. SIEGEL, MD, ("Born to Be *ME*!") previously wrote *Smudge Bunny* (illustrated by Laura J. Bryant), a children's version of Smudge's story; he and Smudge write animal-oriented articles for *laJoie*. A best-selling author, Dr. Siegel's books include *Love, Medicine & Miracles*; *Peace, Love and Healing*; *365 Prescriptions for the Soul*; *101 Exercises for the Soul*; *Love, Magic and Mudpies*; and *Faith, Hope, and Healing*. A retired surgeon, Dr. Siegel developed the Exceptional Cancer Patients therapy program, an integrative approach to cancer that utilizes art, dreams, images, and feelings to bring about changes in an individual's life. For more information, visit Dr. Siegel's website at www.berniesiegelmd.com.

ARTISTS

SUSANNA DEE created the illustration used in the front matter of the book. Susanna has been drawing ever since she can remember, receiving inspiration from nature and her family. While she works primarily in pencil, charcoal, and ink, her realistic style translates well into a variety of media. Susanna lives in California with her husband, children, cats, dogs, and fish.

BEVERLY ENDSLEY created illustrations for "Brown Beauty" (based on a description from R. Lee Terence), "Drowned Rats" (based on photos provided by Nancy LaRoche and O. Earl McCullough), "Emily" (based on a photograph provided by Susan Chernak McElroy), and "The Hidey Box" (based on photos provided by Marie Grosshuesch). An award-winning artist, Beverly is inspired by the old masters and uses techniques and paint preparations popular in Rembrandt's era; she especially enjoys the contrast of light and shadow. Beverly works in oil or watercolor to create wildlife paintings, portraits, and still lifes; her work also includes conté sketches. She lives with her husband and their furred family members in Evergreen, Colorado. Visit her website at www.beverlyendsley.com.

ANDI KLEINMAN created illustrations for "A Real Head-Turner" and "Klezmer" (based on photographs provided by Patrice Pruitte and by Caroline Gilbert and Patrice Pruitte, respectively), "Born to Be *ME*!" (based on photographs provided by Dr. Bernie Siegel), "Frankie's Foible" (based on a description and photograph provided by Bea LeNoir), and for the chapter title pages. Andi's art career spans illustration, advertising, graphic design, and working part-time at her daughter's scrapbook store. She enjoys playing with pencil, pen-and-ink, 3D mixed media, and fabric sculpture; her award-winning art dolls are made of recycled materials. Andi and her family live in Flagstaff, Arizona.

MARY ELLEN WEHRLI created illustrations for "Bunny's Christmas Kingdom: Joy Uncaged" (based on photographs provided by Kimberly Dezelon), "Lobo and Blueberry" (based on photographs provided by Kay Fritzsche), and "Lovable Bobka" (based on photographs provided by Lena Sullivan). Mary Ellen has won awards for both abstract and representational paintings, and her work is displayed in public areas of various US cities. Her preferred medium is acrylic, although she also works in watercolor. Mary Ellen's art includes wall murals inspired by nature, and her designs have been used on puzzles, plates, cards, and as cross-stitch patterns. She currently creates art and teaches in Texas. Visit her website at www.maryellenwehrli.com.

PHOTOGRAPHERS

ELISHA BUNTING is an employee of Best Friends Animal Society and works at the Bunny House.

BEVERLY ENDSLEY, a professional artist, volunteers with the Colorado House Rabbit Society.

VALERIE FOX adopted Baron from Brambley Hedge Rabbit Rescue.

CAROLINE GILBERT is the founder and manager of Rabbit Sanctuary, Inc.

STEPHEN GUIDA is a volunteer with Brambley Hedge Rabbit Rescue.

INGRID HARDING IRVINE is a board member and educator for the Minnesota Companion Rabbit Society.

The late COURTNEY MCCARTY JOHNSON was a volunteer with the House Rabbit Society.

SHARON BARRETT KENNEDY is an artist and art teacher whose wildlife and flower photos have appeared in nature books and magazines.

O. EARL MCCULLOUGH regularly photographs rabbits for the Colorado House Rabbit Society.

CLAY MYERS is a freelance photographer of nature and companion animals.

VELLY OLIVER is a freelance photographer who regularly photographs rabbits for Brambley Hedge Rabbit Rescue.

BILL REED, of Bill Reed Photography, specializes in portraits and lives in the Phoenix metro area.

RAY SILJA has adopted rabbits from Brambley Hedge Rabbit Rescue.

MICHAEL STEIN has adopted rabbits from the Colorado House Rabbit Society.

DEBBY WIDOLF is coordinator of development and outreach for rabbits at Best Friends Animal Society.

ORGANIZATIONS

Representatives of the following organizations responded to my query for information, which became the basis for many of my stories.

House Rabbit Society: Special thanks to Karalee Curry, Beverly Endsley, Kay Fritzsche, Courtney McCarty Johnson, Dr. Jerry LaBonde, Bea LeNoir, and Michael Stein.

The House Rabbit Society (HRS) is an international volunteer-based 501(c)(3) nonprofit organization. Their mission is twofold:

- through their fostering program, volunteers rescue abandoned rabbits and find permanent adoptive homes for them
- through education, they seek to reduce the number of unwanted rabbits—and to improve bunnies' lives—by helping people better appreciate these often misunderstood companion animals.

Since the organization was founded in 1988, HRS foster parents across the US have rescued more than 20,000 rabbits. HRS neuters/spays all incoming rabbits, obtains necessary veterinary care for the bunnies, and attends to their social needs.

Having learned a tremendous amount about rabbits' social, behavioral, and medical requirements (compiled from existing data and necropsy reports), HRS helps veterinarians, humane societies, and individuals living with rabbits to solve behavior and health problems, primarily through the HRS website and membership publication, the *House Rabbit Journal.*

HRS chapters, educators, and foster families are found across the US and, as of this printing, in Canada, Australia, Italy, Hong Kong, and Singapore.

Contact information for the national headquarters: 148 Broadway, Richmond, CA 94804; 510-970-7575.
Website: www.rabbit.org
E-mail addresses: the HRS website provides a list of email addresses, based on the particular issue. In addition to the national organization, HRS chapters can be contacted via e-mail.

Best Friends Animal Society: Special thanks to Elisha Bunting, Chandra Forsythe, Faith Maloney, Lena Sullivan, and Debby Widolf.

Best Friends Animal Society is a 501(c)(3) nonprofit organization whose mission is driven by the simple philosophy that kindness to animals helps build a better world for all of us. The organization's sanctuary is located in southern Utah and is home to approximately 1,700 dogs, cats, horses, birds, and other animals. In addition, Best Friends:

- offers workshops, internships, training programs, and conferences to help individuals, groups, and communities set up and manage their own shelter, rescue, foster, adoption, and spay/neuter programs
- through the online Best Friends Network, helps national and international communities rescue animals in distress and create No More Homeless Pets enclaves
- publishes *Best Friends Magazine.*

Contact information: 5001 Angel Canyon Road, Kanab, UT 84741; 435-644-2001.
Website: www.bestfriends.org
E-mail: rabbits@bestfriends.org and info@bestfriends.org

Brambley Hedge Rabbit Rescue: Special thanks to Terry Bankert, Brock Dezelon, Kimberly Dezelon, Valerie

Fox, Stephen Guida, Erika Smith Royal, Stacey Shirer, and Ray Silja.

Brambley Hedge Rabbit Rescue is an all-volunteer 501(c)(3) nonprofit organization that cares for abused, abandoned, and unwanted domestic rabbits. It is a climate-controlled indoor shelter with supervised open-air play space.

Since 1986, the organization has placed more than 3,000 rabbits with caring adoptive parents. Brambley Hedge assists rabbits in various ways:

- arranging for volunteers to work with county agencies to check on abuse situations
- providing humane traps to the general public for capturing stray rabbits
- offering rabbit-care classes at the Arizona Humane Society
- participating in many Phoenix-area adoptathons to promote humane education and proper rabbit care.

Contact information: P.O. Box 54506, Phoenix, AZ 85078-4506. Hopline 480-443-3990.
Website: www.bhrabbitrescue.org
E-mail: brambley2@bhrabbitrescue.org

MINNESOTA COMPANION RABBIT SOCIETY: Special thanks to Joanna Campbell, Dr. Peg Frank, and Ingrid Harding Irvine.

The Minnesota Companion Rabbit Society (MCRS), established in 2002, is a donation- and member-supported 501(c)(3) nonprofit organization dedicated to improving the lives of companion rabbits; it is staffed primarily by volunteers.

Adoption efforts center on finding permanent homes for rabbits obtained from area shelters and animal control facilities. MCRS places the rabbits in foster homes and addresses physical and/or behavioral issues before arranging permanent adoptions.

Education efforts aim to reduce the number of unwanted bunnies and to improve the lives of rabbits by:

- educating the public about companion rabbits through classes and by response to email and telephone inquiries
- providing training about rabbit care and behavior that is tailored to the specific needs of shelter staff, adoption counselors, and volunteers
- promoting adoption of homeless rabbits through community events and partnerships with retailers
- disseminating rabbit information, news, and event updates through its newsletter, brochures, and handouts, and by participation in special events.

The vision of MCRS is to create a community of rabbit-knowledgeable individuals in Minnesota and to eliminate the need to euthanize adoptable rabbits in St. Paul/Minneapolis and surrounding areas.

Contact information: P.O. Box 390691, Edina, MN 55439. 651-768-9755.
Website: www.mn.companionrabbit.org
E-mail address: info@mn.companionrabbit.org

RABBIT SANCTUARY, INC.: Special thanks to Caroline Gilbert and Patrice Pruitte.

In 1967, Caroline Gilbert established thirty beautiful acres in Simpsonville, South Carolina, as a haven specifically for domestic rabbits. In 1978, she devoted the sanctuary to the work of The Fund for Animals (www.fundforanimals.org) and the refuge continues to be supported by that organization, in conjunction with The Humane Society of the

United States (www.hsus.org). The Rabbit Sanctuary:

- has a unique "Home for Life" policy that ensures a permanent residence for domestic rabbits rescued from local shelters, commercial breeders, laboratories, and conditions deemed neglectful or cruel
- provides medical care, including neutering, and addresses behavioral issues
- offers advice on living with rabbits as companion animals
- publishes the "Rabbit Sanctuary Newsletter," which contains information about the resident rabbits and events at the sanctuary as well as health-related articles
- offers participants in the Adopt-a-Rabbit Sponsorship Program (virtual adoption) a one-year certificate of adoption, a photograph and brief history of the sponsored rabbit, periodic newsletters, and an invitation to attend the sanctuary's annual "Picnic with the Rabbits."

Contact information: P.O. Box 80036, Simpsonville, SC 29680.
Website: www.adopt-a-rabbit.org
E-mail: adoptarabbit@hotmail.com

Resources

Please note that web and e-mail addresses may change, requiring an Internet search for current information.

Included here is a partial listing of rabbit-related resources. For additional references and recent publications, check with local rescue organizations and rabbit-knowledgeable veterinarians; in addition, access reputable websites and resource sections of other books.

READING AND REFERENCE

The *House Rabbit Handbook: How to Live with an Urban Rabbit,* by House Rabbit Society founder Marinell Harriman (Drollery Press), was the first to focus on living with house rabbits. It continues to be an excellent resource and covers pertinent topics about rabbit care and behavior; the book is updated as necessary.

Living with a House Rabbit, by Linda Dykes and Helen Flack (Barron's Educational Series), is a full-color book by two of the founding members of the Rabbit Welfare Association (formerly The British House Rabbit Association); it provides an overview of care and behavior.

The Relaxed Rabbit: Massage for Your Pet Bunny, by professional massage therapist Chandra Moira Beal (book, iUniverse; DVD, La Luna Publishing), shares massage strokes and techniques specifically designed for rabbits.

Stories Rabbits Tell: A Natural and Cultural History of a Misunderstood Creature, by Susan E. Davis and Margo DeMello (Lantern Books), provides an in-depth look at rabbit behavior, offers a comprehensive discussion of the myriad ways in which rabbits (both domestic and wild) are viewed, and discusses how those views impact rabbits' lives, often negatively.

Why Does My Rabbit ...? by rabbit behavior specialist Anne McBride (Souvenir Press Ltd), compares companion rabbits' living conditions to the natural wild environment and discusses how domestic living can distort a rabbit's natural urges and create stress; many behaviors are addressed.

Additional books are available, including:

A House Rabbit Primer by Lucile Moore (Santa Monica Press)

Rabbit Health in the 21st Century by Kathy Smith (iUniverse)

Rabbits for Dummies by Audrey Pavia (Wiley Publishing)

What Your Rabbit Needs by Betsy Sikora Siino (Dorling Kindersley)

Video Resources

These resources—covering a variety of subjects, including getting your first rabbit, introducing rabbits, encouraging exercise, and caring for special-needs bunnies—can be obtained from Drollery Press (www.drollerypress.com).

Health/Medical Journals and Books

Veterinary journals that report current research include *Exotic DVM* and *Journal of Exotic Pet Medicine.*

Books written by veterinarians, covering a wide variety of subjects about rabbit health and behavior, are increasingly available and tend to be relatively easy for laypersons to understand. Examples include:

BSAVA Manual of Rabbit Medicine and Surgery edited by Anna Meredith and Paul Flecknell (British Small Animal Veterinary Association)

Exotic Pet Behavior: Birds, Reptiles, and Small Mammals by Teresa Bradley Bays, Teresa Lightfoot, and Jorg Mayer (Saunders/Elsevier)

Ferrets, Rabbits, and Rodents: Clinical Medicine and Surgery by Katherine E. Quesenberry and James W. Carpenter (Saunders/Elsevier)

The 5-Minute Veterinary Consult: Ferret and Rabbit by Barbara L. Oglesbee (Wiley-Blackwell)

Additional books include *Clinical Radiology of Exotic Companion Mammals* by Vittorio Capello and Angela M. Lennox (Wiley-Blackwell), *Notes on Rabbit Internal Medicine* by Richard A. Saunders and Ron Rees Davies (Blackwell), *Rabbit and Rodent Dentistry Handbook* by Vittorio Capello with Margherita Gracis (Zoological Education Network), *Self-Assessment Colour Review of Rabbit Medicine & Surgery* by Emma Keeble and Anna Meredith (Manson Publishing Ltd), and *Textbook of Rabbit Medicine* by Frances Harcourt-Brown (Butterworth-Heinemann).

MAGAZINES AND OTHER PUBLICATIONS

Individuals interested in reading more about house rabbits can find newsletters and journals/magazines, both in print form and online.

One of the best-known US publications about companion rabbits is the *House Rabbit Journal*, published by the House Rabbit Society (HRS). In the UK, *Rabbiting On* and *Bunny Mad* both emphasize living with a house rabbit.

Many animal rescue groups, including some of those listed on previous pages, provide publications or online newsletters to their members. In addition, e-newsletters from rabbit rescue groups are available; to find them, contact the local/regional group or check the HRS website for a list of other organizations.

Additionally, *Critters USA*, *Rabbits USA*, and *Fur & Feather* cover topics about rabbits.

OTHER READINGS

Human-Animal Relationships

There are increasing numbers of books being written about animals, creating greater understanding of them as sentient beings and exploring their relationship with us. The following list, admittedly not comprehensive, suggests some authors whose writings may be of interest: Allen and Linda Anderson, Jonathan Balcombe, Gene Baur, Diane Beers, Marc Bekoff, Jack Canfield, Karen Davis, Karen Dawn, Margo DeMello, Michael W. Fox, Jane Goodall, Mark Victor Hansen, Leslie Irvine, Amelia Kinkade, Gary Kowalski, Joanne Lauck, Howard F. Lyman, Erik Marcus, Jeffrey Moussaieff Masson, Susan Chernak McElroy, Charles Patterson, Irene Pepperberg, Norm Phelps, Mary Lou Randour, Tom Regan, Allen Schoen, Matthew Scully, Kenneth Shapiro, Peter Singer, Penelope Smith, Kim Stallwood, Kristin von Kreisler, Michael Tobias, and Will Tuttle.

Death, Dying, and Grief

The loss of a companion animal can be traumatic, especially when family members and friends do not understand the depth of the grief. Hearing about others' experiences with this kind of loss can provide assistance and comfort. Emily Stuparyk wrote *When Only the Love Remains* after the death of her beloved rabbit. Other authors who deal with the issue of companion animal loss are: Rita Reynolds in *Blessing the Bridge*, Dr. Bernie Siegel in *Buddy's Candle*, and Allen and Linda Anderson in *Saying Goodbye to Your Angel Animals*. In addition, Kim Sheridan writes about animals and the afterlife, and books by Julia Harris and Gary Kowalski offer solace and support.

INTERNET RESOURCES

Health

- American Holistic Veterinary Medical Association: www.ahvma.org
- Celebrating Rabbits: www.celebratingrabbits.com
- House Rabbit Society: www.rabbit.org (especially the links to Care, Behavior, Health, FAQS, and Chapters)
- MediRabbit: www.medirabbit.com
- Morfz: www.morfz.com
- Rabbit Adoption and Information Network: www.lagomorphs.com
- Veterinary Partner: www.veterinarypartner.com

Rescue Organizations

There are many good rabbit rescue organizations; unfortunately, it is impossible to list them all here, and any list will periodically change. The House Rabbit Society maintains one of the most complete listings of national and international rabbit rescue groups. Reference the previous pages for some other organizations that have links to good resources. In addition to checking for information on those websites, an Internet search for *rabbit rescue organizations* will help get you started. If you do not have access to the Web, perhaps the reference librarian at your local library can provide assistance.

Additional Online Options

The Web offers many options for obtaining and sharing information. Listening to a lecture, participating in a discussion, viewing or posting photos and videos, and communicating with people in other countries are just some of the ways that individuals share information about rabbits. Ask members of the local rescue group for information about good sites. In addition, the House Rabbit Society website provides some links and indexes to help get you started.

PRODUCTS AND SUPPLIES

Below are some US suppliers of rabbit-related items. Whether you live in the US or in another country, check with your local rescue organization, other rabbit lovers, and online for additional suppliers.

American Pet Diner: HC 62, Box 62505, Eureka, NV 89316. 775-237-5570, 800-656-2691. www.americanpetdiner.com

Bunny Bytes: P.O. Box 69733, Seattle, WA 98168. 888-563-9300 (A fax phone; it will beep before the voice message.) www.bunnybytes.com

Bunny Heaven: PMB 262, 16 Mt. Bethel Rd., Warren, NJ 07059-5604. 732-563-0177. www.bunnyheaven.com

BunnyLuv Essentials: 16742 Stagg Street, #104, Van Nuys, CA 91406. 818-988-4488. www.bunnyluv.com

The Busy Bunny: P.O. Box 1023, San Bruno, CA 94066-7023. 650-652-5930. www.busybunny.com

House Rabbit Resource Network: P.O. Box 152432, Austin, TX 78715. 512-444-3277. www.rabbitresource.org

House Rabbit Society (many chapters sell items): www.rabbit.org

Leith Petwerks, Inc.: P.O. Box 13520, Salem, OR 97309. 503-362-9457 or 800-956-3576. www.leithpetwerks.com

Oxbow Animal Health: 29012 Mill Road, Murdock, NE 68407. 800-249-0366. www.oxbowanimalhealth.com

Rabbit Adoption and Information Network (maintains a list of suppliers): www.lagomorphs.com

24 Carrot Lane: 1839 Ygnacio Valley Road, #285, Walnut Creek, CA 94598. 925-944-1967. www.24carrotlane.com

SERVICES

Guardian Campaign: In Defense of Animals, 3010 Kerner Blvd., San Rafael, CA 94901. 415-388-9641. www.guardiancampaign.com

Professional Pet Transports, Inc.: 59154 Trafton Lane, John Day, OR 97845. www.pro-pet-transports.com

CRUELTY-FREE PRODUCTS AND DISSECTION ALTERNATIVE PROGRAMS

Several organizations offer informative shopping guides to help consumers choose cruelty-free products that have not been tested on animals. Many of the groups also provide workbooks, software, and models to help promote effective learning about animal biology and anatomy without the need to kill and/or perform dissections on animals.

American Anti-Vivisection Society (AAVS): 801 Old York Rd., Suite 204, Jenkintown, PA 19046. 800-SAY-AAVS (729-2287); 215-887-0816. www.aavs.org

National Anti-Vivisection Society (NAVS): 53 W Jackson Blvd., Suite 1552, Chicago, IL 60604. 800-888-NAVS (6287); 312-427-6065. www.navs.org

New England Anti-Vivisection Society (NEAVS): 333 Washington St., Suite 850, Boston, MA 02108. 617-523-6020. www.neavs.org (Contact the Ethical Science and Education Coalition at that same address and telephone number for free science education tools.)

People for the Ethical Treatment of Animals (PETA): 501 Front St., Norfolk, VA 23510. 757-622-7382. www.peta.org

Physicians Committee for Responsible Medicine (PCRM): 5100 Wisconsin Ave. NW, Ste. 400, Washington, DC 20016-4131. 202-686-2210. www.pcrm.org

PCRM is a nonprofit organization working toward compassionate and effective medical practice, research, and health promotion.

Index

A

Abandonment (see also Prey animals), 14, 46, 50, 54, 100, 105, 110, 119-120
- Misconceptions about, 105, 129
- Reasons for, 59, 120, 129
- Results of, 54, 59, 62, 104, 106-107, 110, 129

Abbott, Cheryl Rosemary, 132, 146
Abuse/mistreatment, 2, 23, 27, 34, 37, 43, 59, 61, 64, 89-90, 96, 101, 115
- As a result of improper handling 41, 95, 128

Acrobatics, 13, 19, 69, 75, 90
Adenocarcinoma (see Cancer)
Adolescence, 22, 59, 107-108, 114
Adoption (see New rabbit)
Aggression (see also Biting; Defensive actions), 14, 31
- Reasons for, 2, 29-30, 32-34, 45, 59, 114, 126, 127

Allergies, 128, 129
American Board of Veterinary Practitioners (ABVP), 145
Analgesic (pain medication), 141, 142, 143
Anesthesia (see also Medical Care), 141
Animal shelters, 63, 129
Antibiotics (see Medication)
Anti-inflammatory non-steroidal medication (see Medication)
Anxiety (see also Fear), 11-12, 13, 31
Arthritis, 4, 141
Association of Exotic Mammal Veterinarians (AEMV), 145, 147

B

Baby rabbits (see also Reproduction), 50, 53, 54, 60, 61, 96, 99, 112
- Nest building & Nursing, 112-114
- Protecting from predators, 114

Backyard, 23, 27
Bacterial disease screening, 141
Baskets, 125
Bathing (see also Fur), 122
Behaviors, instinctive, 13, 22, 45, 59, 75, 105, 109, 126, 127
Best Friends Animal Society, 14, 32, 149
Binkies (see Acrobatics)
Bird, rabbit friendship with, 83
Biting (see also Aggression; Defensive actions), 8, 14, 62, 79
- Lunging (as if to bite), 2, 82, 116, 127
- Reasons for, 2, 22, 49, 51, 116, 127

Bladder stones or sludge (diagnosis by x-ray), 141
Blind spots, 49
Bloodwork, 141
Bonding rabbits (see also Companionship; Social nature), 10-11, 14, 28-31, 62, 79, 83
Boxes, 29, 81, 125
Brambley Hedge Rabbit Rescue, 37, 50, 112, 114, 149-150
Breathing difficulty (see Respiratory system)
Breeding, selective, xx, 49, 105
Brushing (see Fur)
Bunny-proofing (see also Chewing; Digging; Teeth), 107-109, 125, 127, 135

C

Cages (see also Housing; Hutches), xx, 2, 3, 125
Cancer (carcinoma; see also Medical care)
    Mammary gland, 116-117, 118
    Uterine, 118
    Testicular, 118
    Other, 118
Cardiovascular disease (heart disease), 78, 141
Care of rabbits, 124-125, 127-130
Carnivals, 99
Cat, rabbit friendship with, 19-20, 83, 93-94
Cavy (Guinea pig), rabbit friendship with, 83
Cecotropes, 125, 142
Cephalosporins (see Medication)
Cheek teeth (see Teeth)
Chewing (see also Bunny-proofing; Teeth), 22, 59, 107-108, 109, 125, 126, 127, 135
Children and rabbits, 41, 91, 95, 126-130, 132-139
Chin rubbing, 71
Classroom rabbit (see School/classroom rabbit)
Clay litter, 125
Cleaning a rabbit (see also Fur), 122
Clindamycin (see Medication)
Combing (see Fur)
Communication (see also Social nature), 22, 45, 134
Companionship (see also Bonding rabbits; Communication; Death/loss; Social nature)
    Multiple rabbits, 8, 11, 13, 31, 35, 40-41, 48-49, 69, 71, 74, 90-91, 94, 108, 117, 127
    "Warren," domestic, xx
    With humans, xx-xxi, xxiv, 17, 20-22, 48, 53, 58-59, 71, 74, 75, 95, 116, 124
    Creating trust, 7, 32, 35, 38, 45, 51, 116, 134
    With other animals (see also Cat; Dog), 83
Condo (see Cages; Housing)
County fairs (see Carnivals)
Crepuscular, 127
Cultural views of rabbits, 18, 63, 126

D

Deafness, 6-7, 9, 11
Death/loss, 30, 34, 36, 49, 54, 94
Defensive actions (see also Aggression; Biting), 14, 32, 35, 45, 49, 51, 115-116, 127
Dehydration, preventing, 137
Dental (see Teeth)
Depression/despondency, 13, 34, 36, 49, 54, 94, 129
Diet (see also Feeding), 77, 125, 128, 141
Digestive system (see also Feeding), 21, 128, 142
    Gastrointestinal stasis, 2, 7, 141
Digging (see also Bunny-proofing), 17, 22, 59, 109, 125, 126
    Digging box, 125
Disease (see also Medical care)
    Cancer, 118
    Cardiovascular (heart), 78, 141
    Dental, 141, 144, 145
    Hepatic (liver) lipidosis, 77, 78, 141
    Osteoporosis, 41
Dog, rabbit friendship with, 15, 83

E

Easter gifts, rabbits as, 54, 59
    Make Mine Chocolate!™ campaign, 59
Electrical cords (see Bunny-proofing)
Emergency care (see Medical care)
Erythromycin (see Medication)
Exercise, 41, 125, 127, 135
Exotic mammal, rabbit as (see Veterinarians)

F

Fasting (see Medical care)
Fear (see also Anxiety; Predators; Stress), 13, 38, 46, 54, 99, 110, 111, 127
    Physical displays of, 24, 25, 26, 32, 42, 51, 62, 68, 92, 108
    Results of, 27, 32-34, 99
Fecal pellets, 122, 137, 140

Feeding (see also Diet; Digestive system; Medical care)
Babies, special care for, 61, 96, 99
Fasting before surgery, 143
Fiber, 127, 128, 144
Food pellets, 77, 125, 128
Hay, 77, 78, 125, 127, 128, 144
Syringe-feeding, 143
Vegetables, leafy green, 77, 125, 128
Water, 14, 34, 46, 125, 137, 143
Feet, damaged, 2, 27
Feet, thumping, 4-5, 7, 11, 20, 79
Ferrets, 83
Fiber (see Feeding)
Fighting (see Aggression)
Fox, Dr. Michael W., xxi, 146
Friendship (see Companionship)
Fund for Animals, The, 150
Fur, 50, 112
Allergies, 128, 129
Angora (long, silky hair), 6, 25, 128
Grooming/cleaning, 122, 124, 128
Mites, 64, 89
Spot cleaning fur, 122

G

Grass hay (see Feeding)
Grass mats, 125
Greens (leafy vegetables; see Feeding)
Grieving (see also Companionship; Death/loss), 34, 36
Grooming (see Fur)
Guardian (as preferred term for "owner"), xviii, 124
Guinea pig (cavy), rabbit friendship with, 83

H

Handling (see also Children and rabbits), 2, 38, 39, 41, 77, 95, 124, 128
Hay, grass (see Feeding)
Head tilt (due to neurological damage), 37, 38, 39
Heart disease (cardiovascular disease), 78, 141
Heat exhaustion (heat stress), 94, 96, 99
Heat, supplemental, for surgery, 143
Hepatic (liver) lipidosis, 77, 78
Holiday concerns, 88
House Rabbit Society, 10, 43, 59, 67, 94, 149
Housing (see also Cages; Hutches; Litter box), 3, 125, 127, 135-137
Wire flooring, 2-3, 27, 125
Humane Society of the United States, The, 150
Hutches (see also Cages; Housing), 23, 27

I

Illness (see also Disease; Medical care), 95, 99, 128
Incisors (see Teeth)
Infection, 141, 145
Inflammation, 141
Injections, 66, 142, 143
Injury (see also Medical care), 27, 41, 95, 99, 127, 128
Intelligence, 15, 17, 22, 53, 56, 129
Interaction, social (see Companionship; Social nature)
Intestinal stasis or obstruction (diagnosis by x-ray), 141
Instinctive behaviors (see Behaviors, instinctive)

J

Jumping (see also Acrobatics), 41

K

Kidney disease or stones (diagnosis by x-ray), 141

L

Language (see Communication)
LaRoche, Nancy, 42, 119
Leafy green vegetables, 125, 128
Lennox, Dr. Angela M., 105, 144, 146
Lincomycin (see Medication)
Litter box (see also Housing; Spay/neuter), 17, 125, 137
Litter types, 2, 125
Liver disease, 77, 78

Living space (see Housing)
Loneliness (see Depression/despondency)
Lymphatic system, and cancer, 118

M

Make Mine Chocolate!™ campaign, 59
McElroy, Susan Chernak, xxiv, 18, 147
Medical care (see also Disease; Medication; Overweight; Teeth; Veterinarians), 43, 58, 65, 71-73, 76, 96, 128, 140-143
    Anesthesia, 141
    Companionship, importance of, 75, 142
    Emergency care, 60, 65, 90, 101, 105, 122
    Fasting before surgery, 143
    Fluids, subcutaneous, 143
    Illness/injury, hiding signs of, 128, 139, 140, 142
    Illness/injury, signs of, 1-2, 21, 37, 43, 47, 60, 61, 64, 76, 89, 96, 101, 112, 116, 140
    Injections, 143
    Mites, ear, 64
    Mites, fur, 64, 76, 89
    Parasites, 50, 141
    Sedation, 141, 145
    Surgical issues, 117, 142-143
    Tests, diagnosis, 141
Medication
    Antibiotics, 21, 142
    Pain relief, 142
    Penicillin, injectable, 65, 66, 68, 142
    Penicillin, oral, 142
Minnesota Companion Rabbit Society, 115, 150
Mites (see Medical care)
Molars (see Teeth)

N

Neglect (see Abuse/mistreatment)
Nest building, 112
Neuter (see Reproduction; Spay/neuter)
New rabbit, 63, 123
Night droppings (see Cecotropes)
Nipping (see also Biting), 22
Non-steroidal anti-inflammatory drugs (NSAIDs; see Medication)

O

Obesity (see also Medical care), 27, 76, 77, 78
Opioid, 142
Osteoporosis, 41
Overpopulation (see Reproduction)
Overweight (see also Medical care), 27, 78

P

Pain, 2, 4, 5, 58, 65, 101, 141, 142, 143, 144
Pain medication (analgesic), 141, 142, 143
Pairing rabbits (see Bonding rabbits)
Pellets, fecal (see Fecal pellets)
Pellets, food (see Feeding)
Penicillin (see Medication)
Personality/true nature (see also Companionship; Prey animals; Social nature), xx, 7, 8-9, 22, 27, 28, 45, 84-88, 91, 107-108, 112-114, 117, 126, 129
    Displays of, 13, 15-17, 20, 22, 26, 35, 40, 44, 51, 53, 56, 58-59, 61-62, 63, 71, 73-74, 78, 82, 89, 90, 108, 120-121
Petting, 137
Petting zoos (see Carnivals)
Physical impairment, 2, 4, 6, 27, 37, 38, 76
Physiology (see also Injury), 41
Play (see also Companionship; Social nature), 125
Predators (see also Prey animals), 14, 19, 27, 46, 54, 55, 83, 105, 110, 126
    Protecting babies from, 114
Pregnancy, 53
Prey animals (see also Abandonment; Predators), 13, 105, 110, 126, 127
    Illness/injury, hiding signs of (see Medical care)
    Psychology of, 13, 45, 123, 126
Punishing a rabbit, 17, 22
Purchasing (see New rabbit)
Purring, tooth (see Teeth)

R

Rabbit Sanctuary, 23, 47, 90, 96, 101, 150-151
Radiographs (x-rays), 141
Reproduction (see also Adolescence; Baby rabbits; Spay/neuter), 50, 53
Rescue (see also Abandonment), 14, 46-47, 54-55, 62, 64, 100-104, 106, 110-112, 119, 129
Respiratory system (see also Medical care), 76, 140, 141
Routine, importance of, 127, 138

S

Safety (see Bunny-proofing)
School/classroom rabbit, xxiii, xxiv, 1, 2, 32, 34, 89-90, 91, 126-130, 132-139
Scissors, use in grooming, 122
Sedation, 141, 145
Sexual maturity (see Adolescence; Reproduction; Spay/neuter)
Shedding (molting; see also Fur), 128
Shelters, animal, 63, 129
Siegel, Dr. Bernie, xxiv, 54, 147
Sight (see Vision)
Signs of illness/injury (see Medical Care)
Social nature (see also Communication; Companionship; Personality/true nature), xx, 11, 22, 31, 75, 83, 124, 129
Spay/neuter (see also Adolescence; Reproduction), 53, 114, 118, 124
  Benefits of, 17, 114, 124
Splay leg, 6
Spraying, territorial, 114
Stress (see also Fear; Predators; School/classroom rabbit), 12, 13, 24, 25, 88, 99, 103, 127, 142
Surgery (see also Medical Care), 142-143, 145
Syringe-feeding (see Feeding)

T

Teeth (see also Bunny-proofing; Chewing; Medical care), 127, 141, 144-145
  Abscess, 64, 65, 66, 71-73, 144
  Incisors, eating without, 104-105, 145
  Problems, treatment of, 105, 144-145
  Purring, tooth, 38, 44, 51
Testicles (see also Spay/neuter), 114
Testing, product, rabbits as victims of, xx
Thumping (see Feet)
Tilmicosin (see Medication)
Timothy hay (see Feeding)
Training, 17, 134
Trans-species illness, 128
Trauma, emotional, 24, 25
Travel, 99

U

Ultrasound, 141
Urinary stones or sludge (diagnosis by x-ray), 141
Urine burn, 4, 5, 37, 64, 76

V

Vegetables (see Feeding)
Veterinarians (see also Medical care), 53, 114, 124, 128, 140-143, 144-145
  Rabbits as exotics, 99, 128, 145
Vinegar, use in cleaning, 125
Vision, 7, 11, 49
  Biting, as related to, 49
  Scanning, 23, 49

W

Warren, xx
Weight (see Medical care; Obesity; Weight loss)
Weight loss, 144

X

X-rays (radiographs), 141